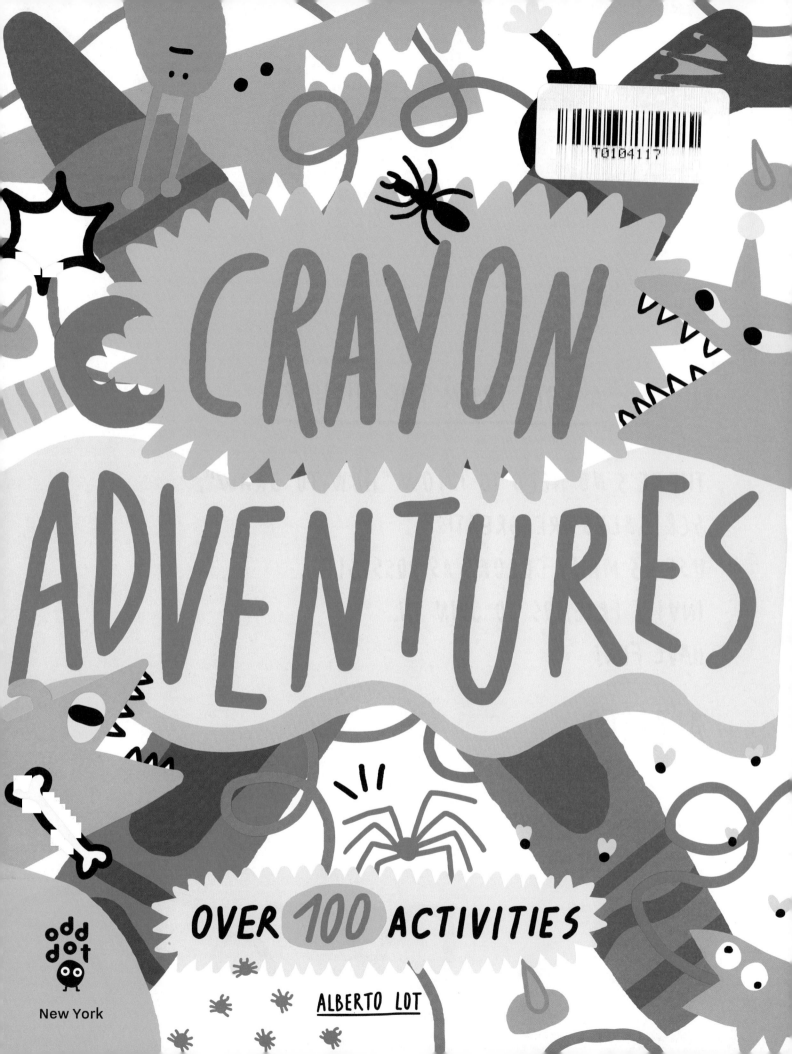

CRAYON ADVENTURES

OVER 100 ACTIVITIES

ALBERTO LOT

odd dot

New York

A NOTE FROM THE AUTHOR:

THERE'S NO NEED TO KNOW "HOW TO DRAW".
SCRIBBLES ARE GREAT!
USE AS MANY COLORS AS POSSIBLE.
INVITE FRIENDS TO JOIN IN.
HAVE FUN!

ALBERTO

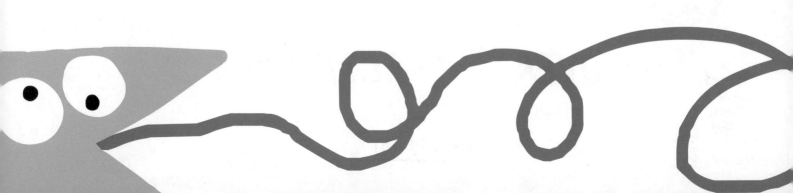

CRAYON ADVENTURE GROUND RULES:

* FILL THE PAGES WITH YOUR SCRIBBLES.
* READ THE RULES IN EACH ADVENTURE,
  OR MAKE UP YOUR OWN!
* IF YOU THINK THERE IS A BETTER WAY TO DO IT, DO IT!
* DISCOVER ALL THE ADVENTURES ACROSS THE PAGES.

READY, SET...

Crocodiles have bad breath every day! Draw what it smells like!

Draw the magical energy coming from the hands!

2 PLAYERS

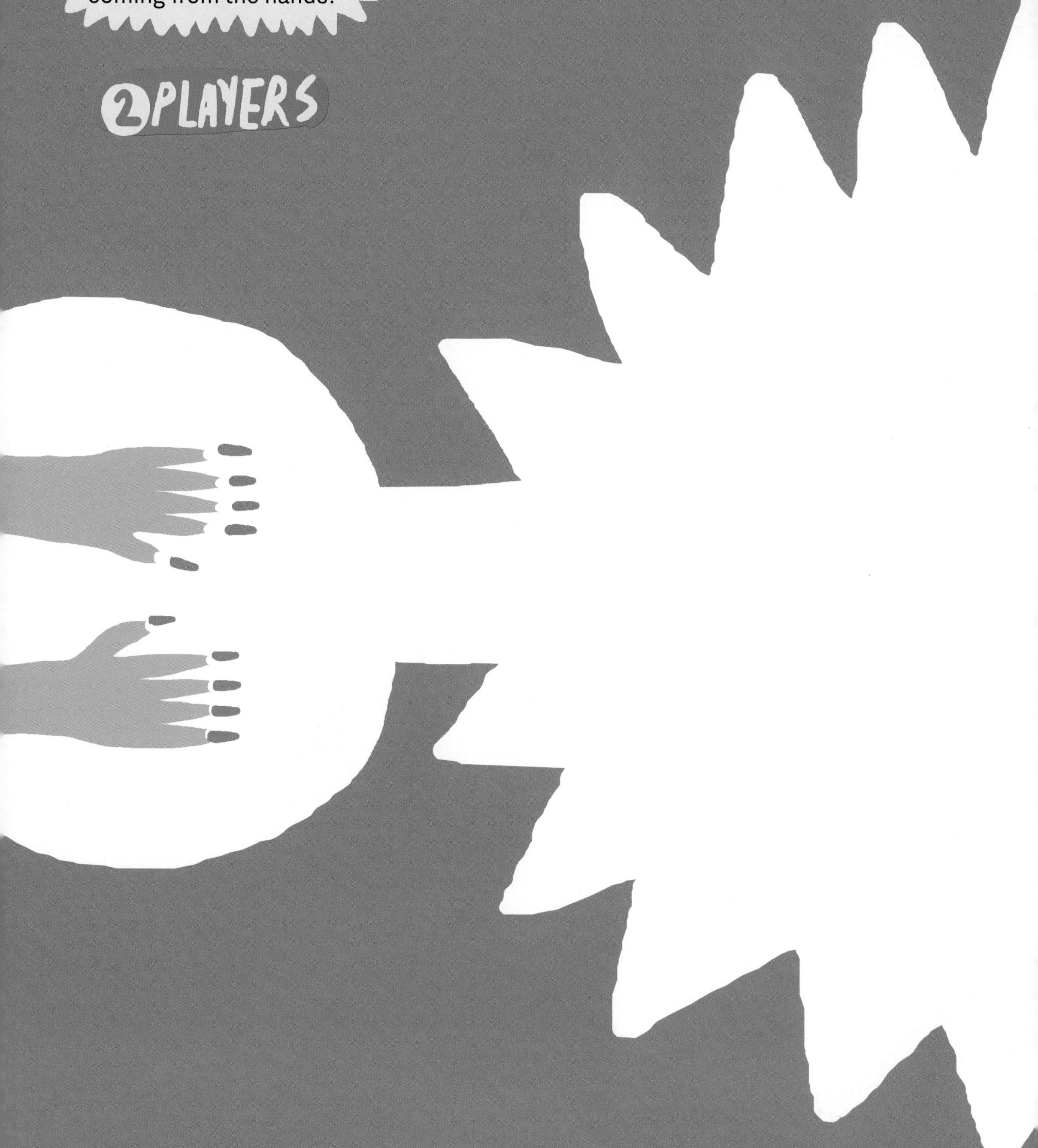

Draw the magical energy coming from the hands!

Different hands have different powers!

Who will win?

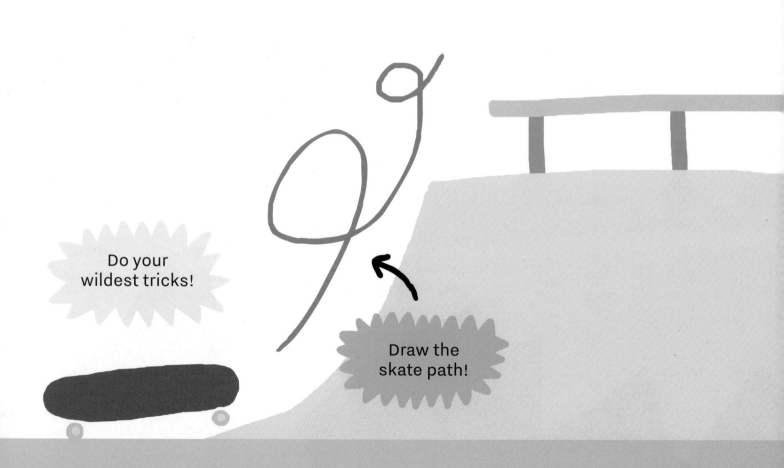

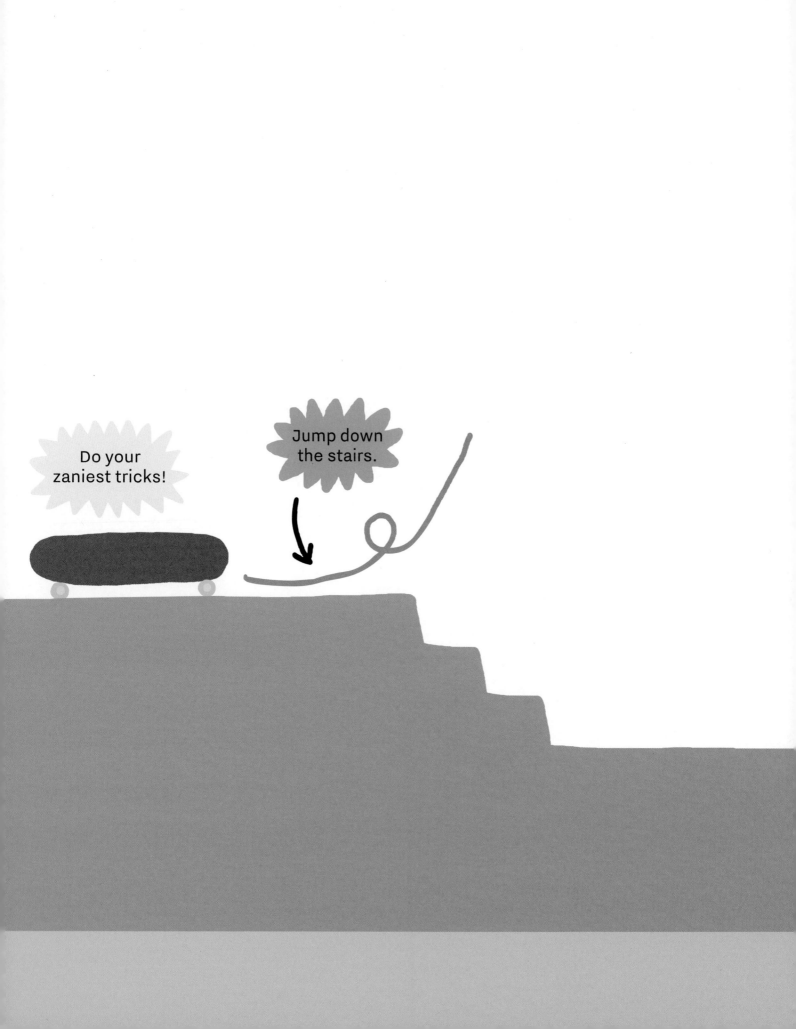

Do your most
over-the-top tricks!

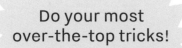

Beware the crocodile!

Draw her shell!
Make it fashion, please.
(Can you SNAIL it?)

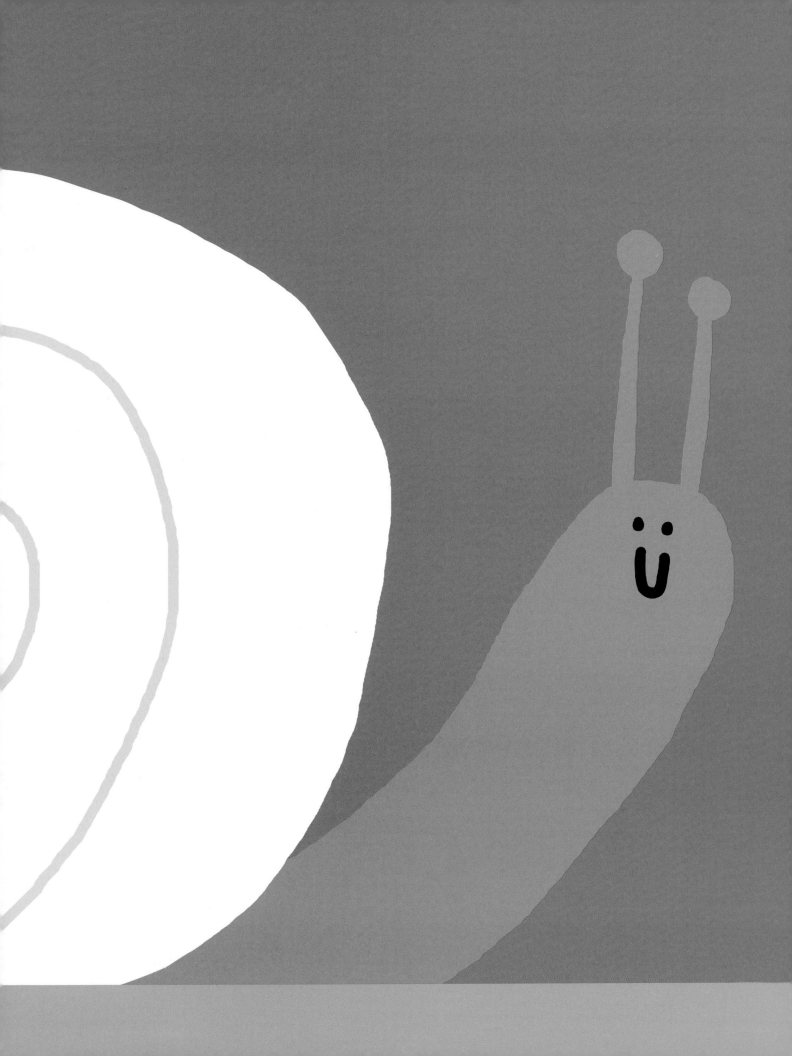

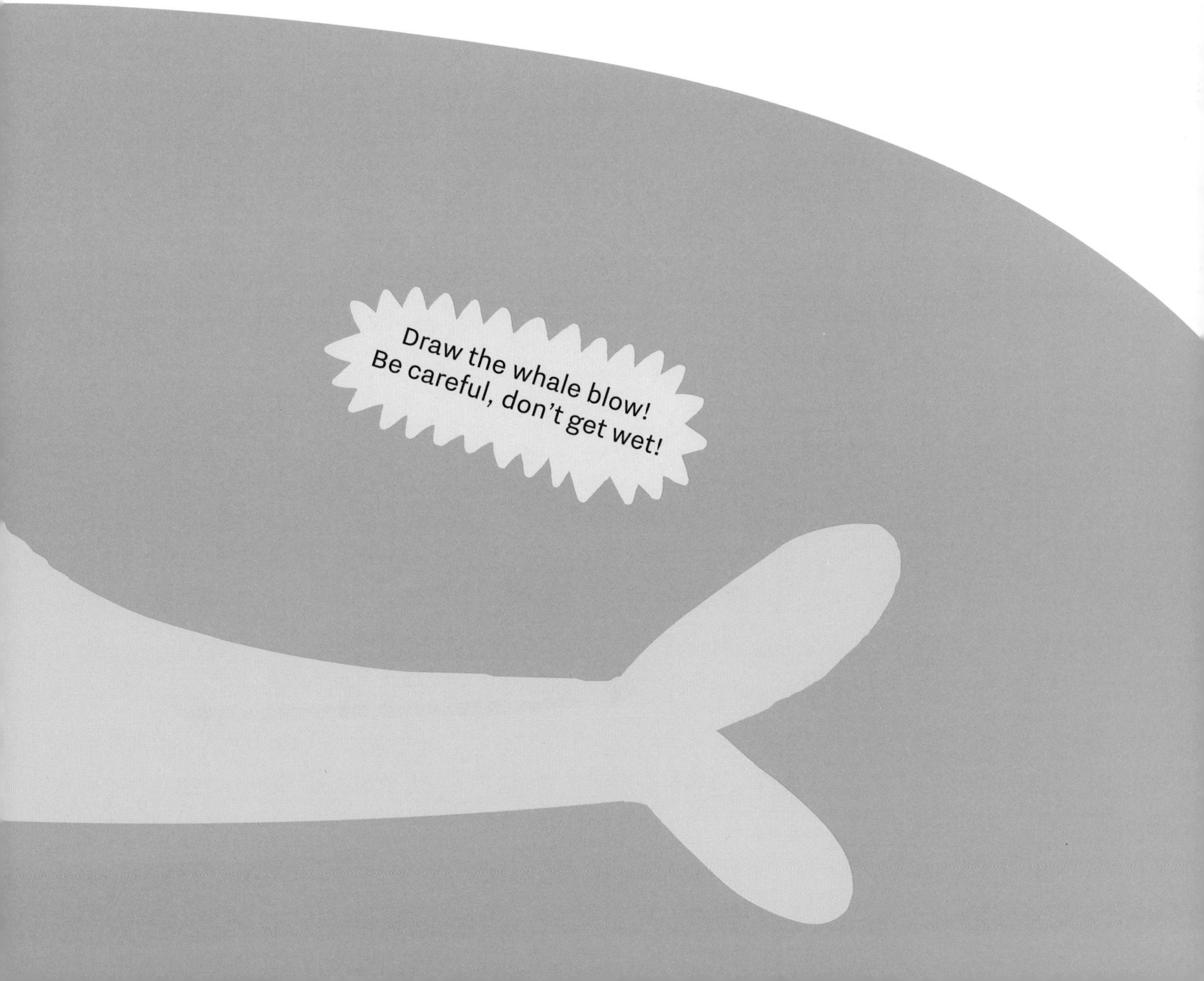
Draw the whale blow!
Be careful, don't get wet!

This is a blow war!

Decorate the snake!

Watch out! This snake is long.
You'd better turn the page!

Draw the plant climbing everywhere!

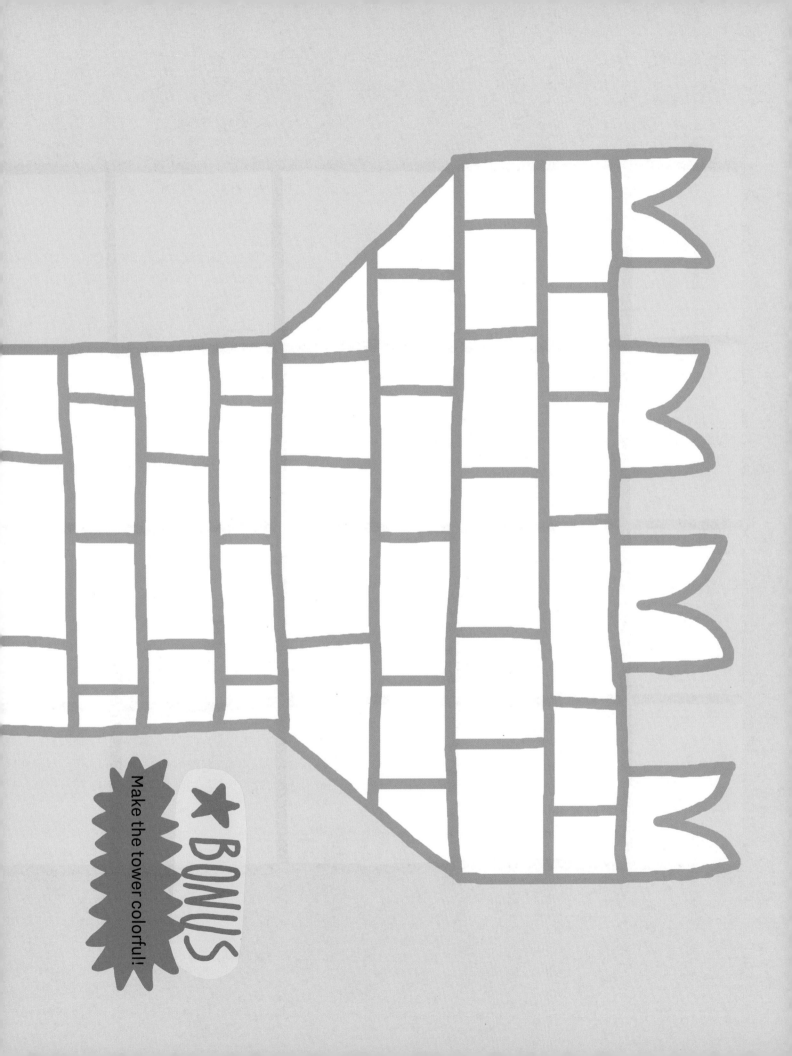

★ BONUS

Make the tower colorful!

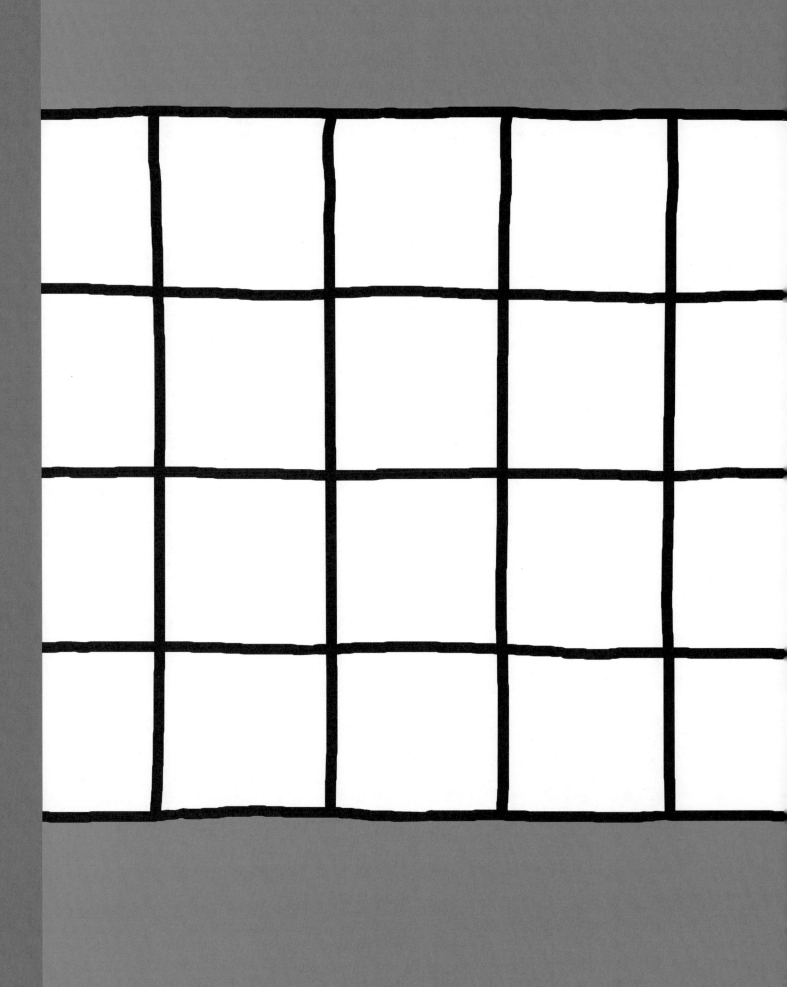

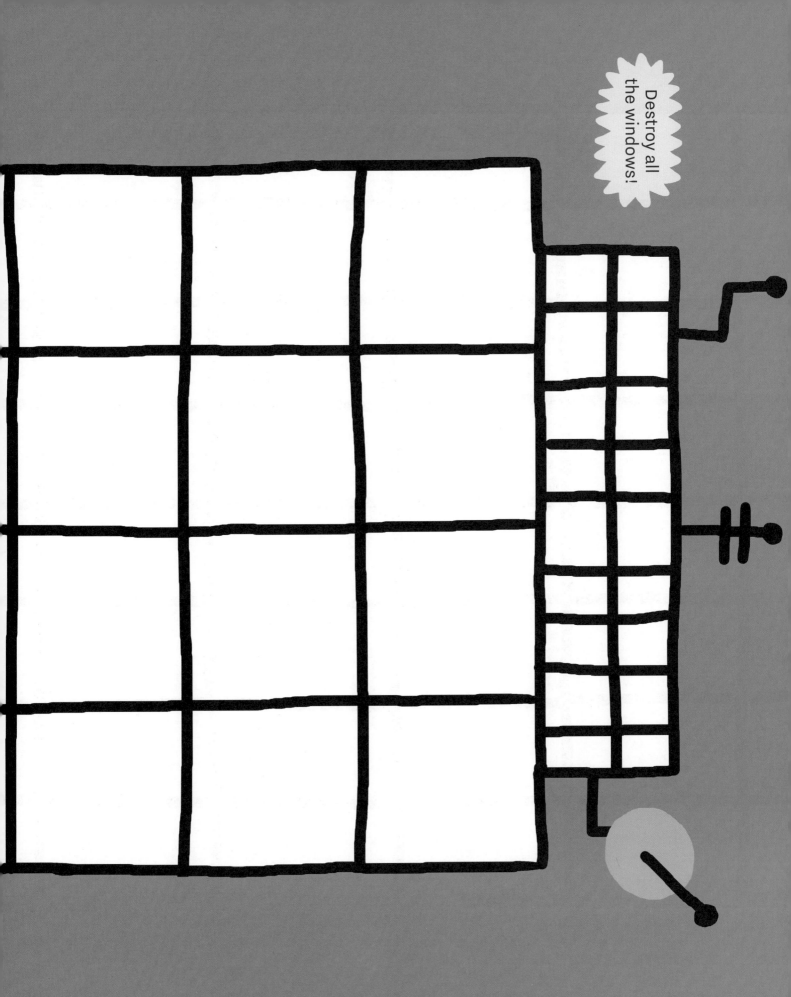

★ BONUS
Crash every window!

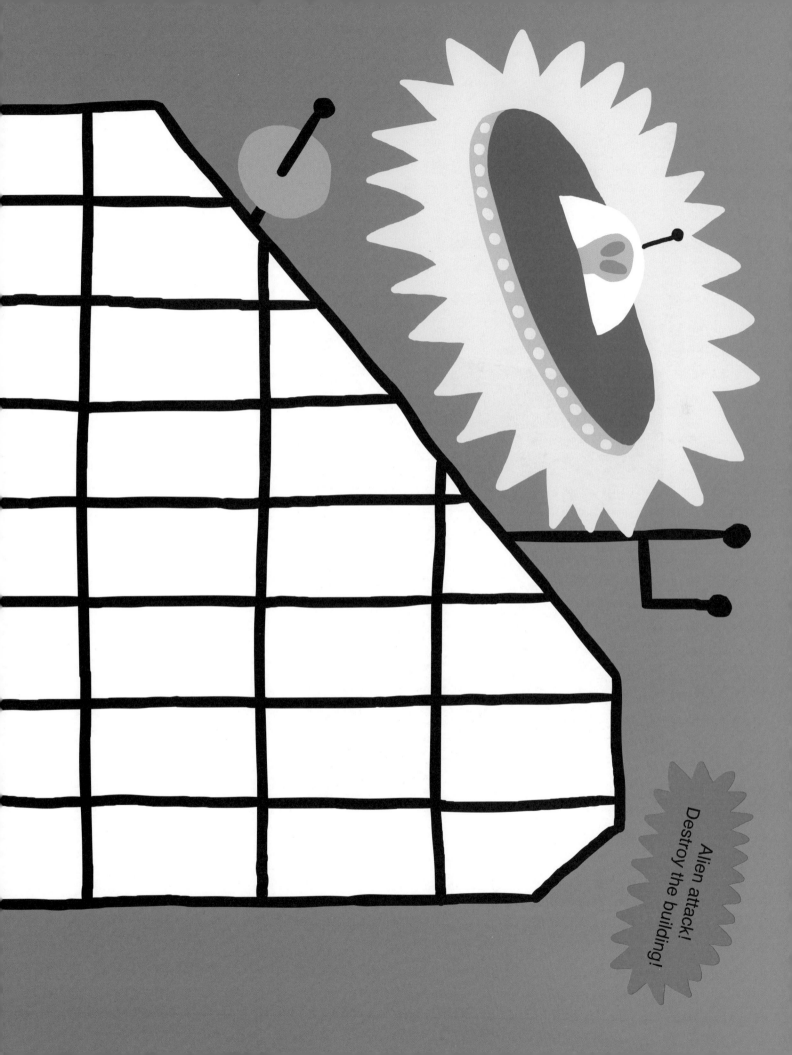

Alien attack! Destroy the building!

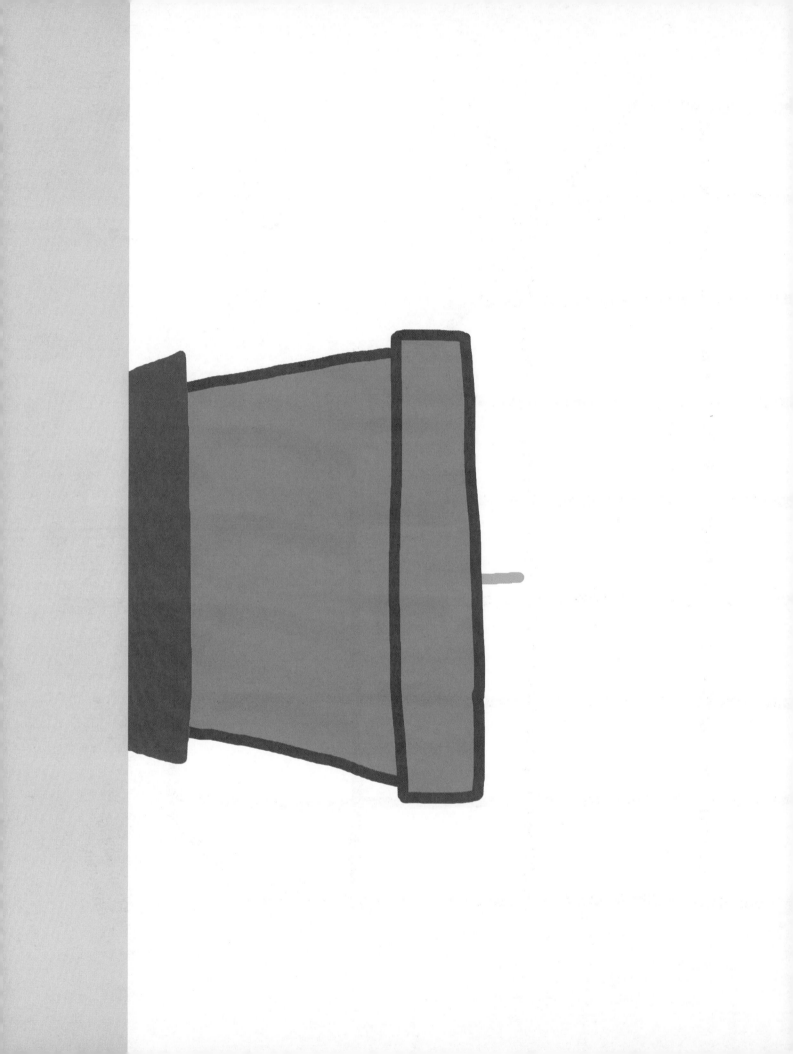

Draw the plant growing.

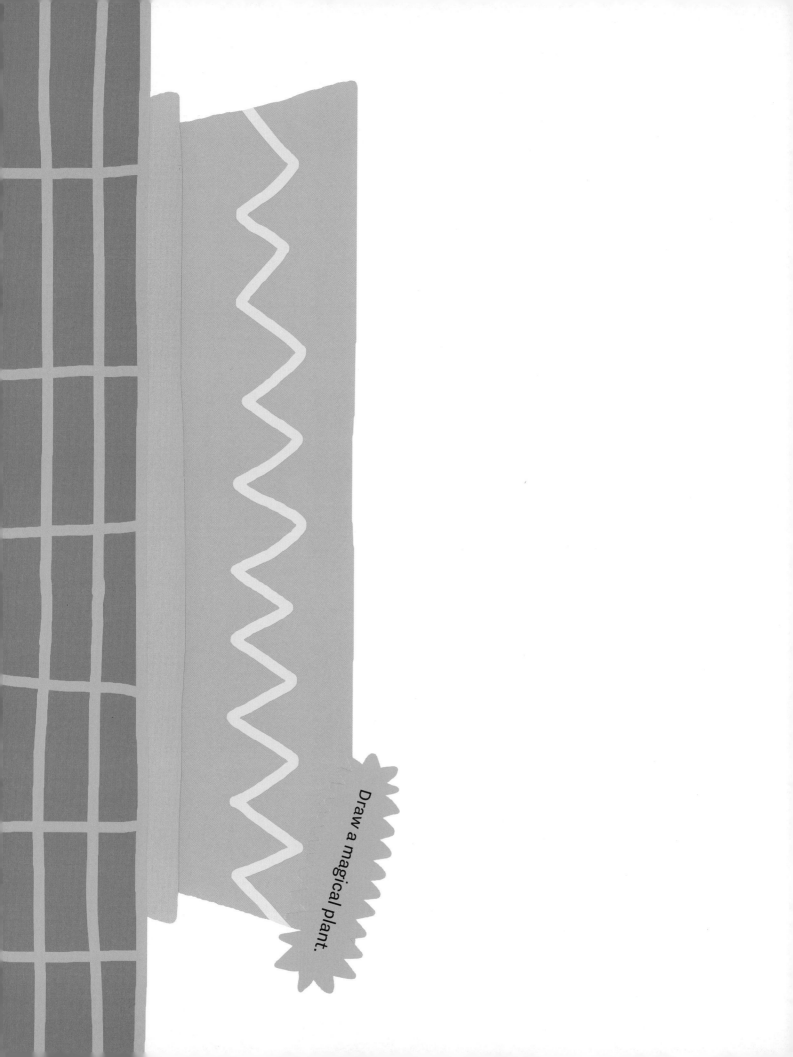

Draw a magical plant.

The pot is overflowing!

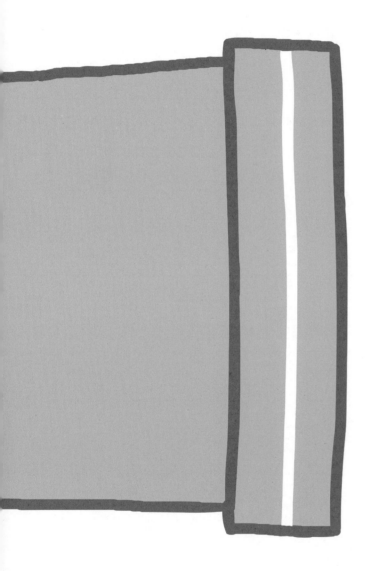

★ BONUS

Add some flowers!

★ BONUS

Add some flowers!

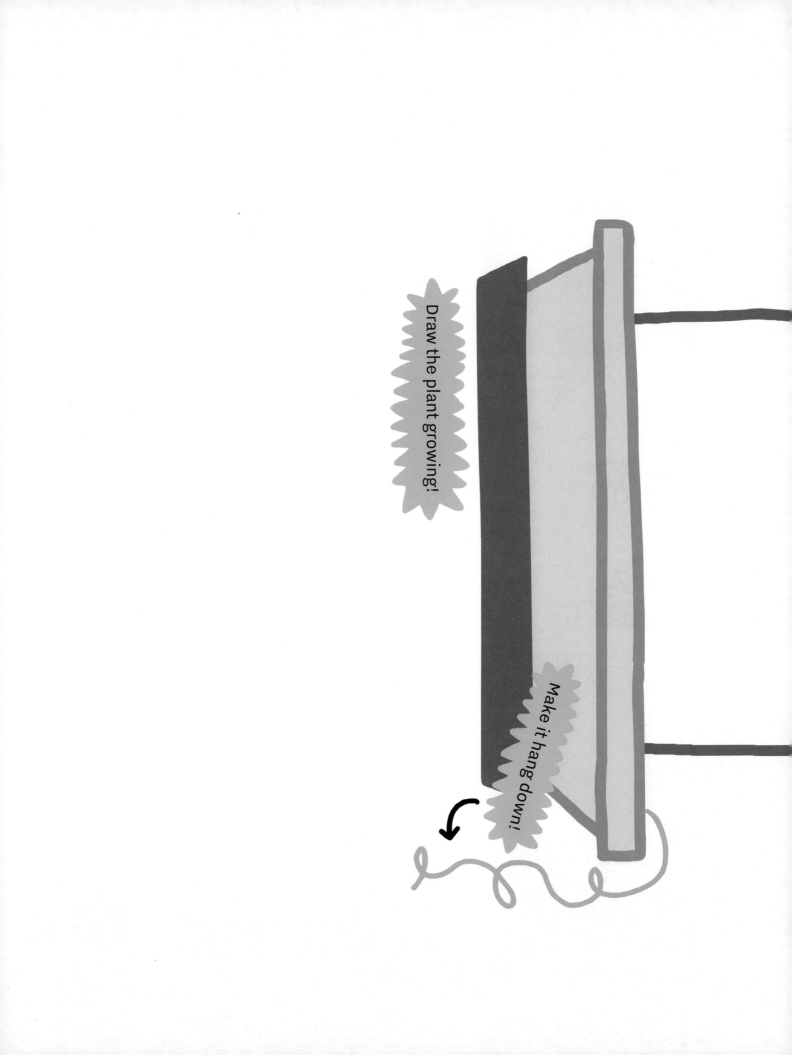

It's a dragon fight!

②PLAYERS

It's a multi-headed dragon fight!

Fireworks!
Draw the explosions!

Draw the most colorful and powerful explosion you can imagine!

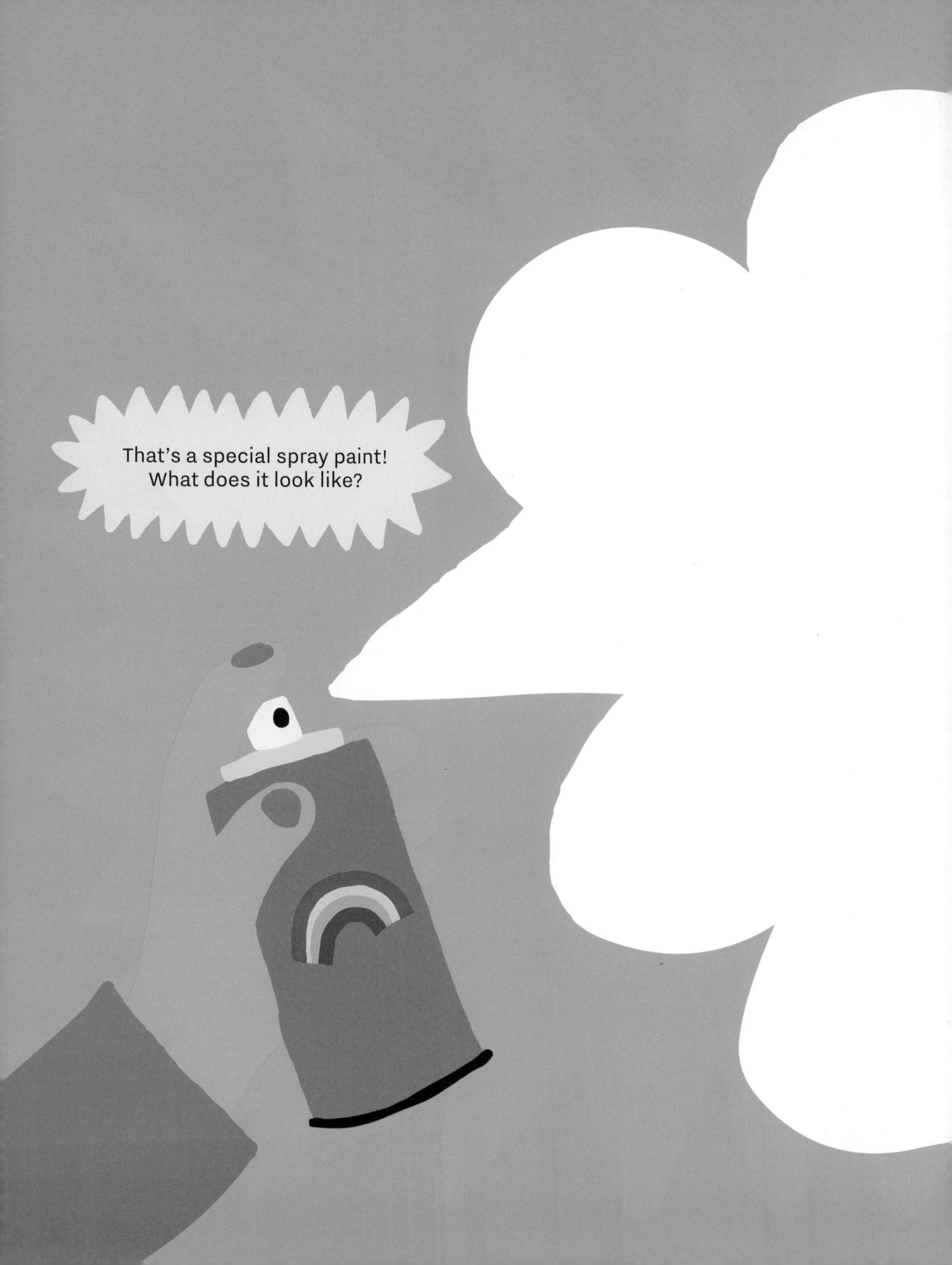
That’s a special spray paint!
What does it look like?

It's a spray war!

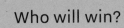

Who will win?

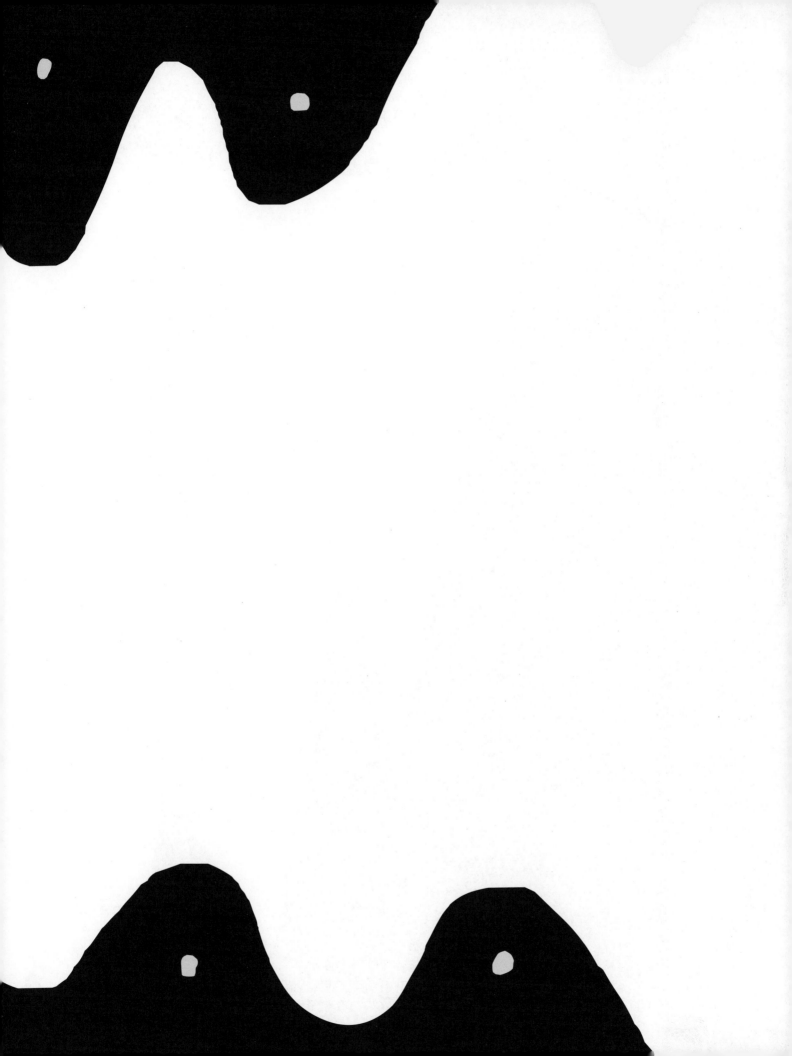

This tri-jetpack has blasted off! Draw the propulsion!

Draw each plane's trajectory!

Try not to crash them
into each other!
(If they do, draw the explosion!)

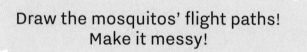

Draw the mosquitos' flight paths!
Make it messy!

How noisy is a mosquito?
Draw its flight path as it flies
by (or into!) the ear!

Look at those knights' helmets. Make them shocking!

Design the helmets you'd want to wear!

What's coming out of the monster's mouth? Draw it!

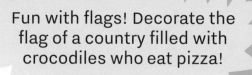

Fun with flags! Decorate the flag of a country filled with crocodiles who eat pizza!

Fun with flags!
Decorate the flag
as you wish!

The mozzarella is melting!

Use a white crayon to draw as many mozzarella threads as you can!

★ BONUS

Add any extra toppings you like!

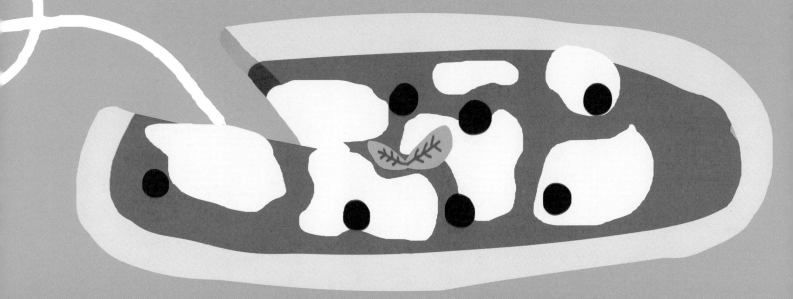

Buildings are serious.
Make them silly!

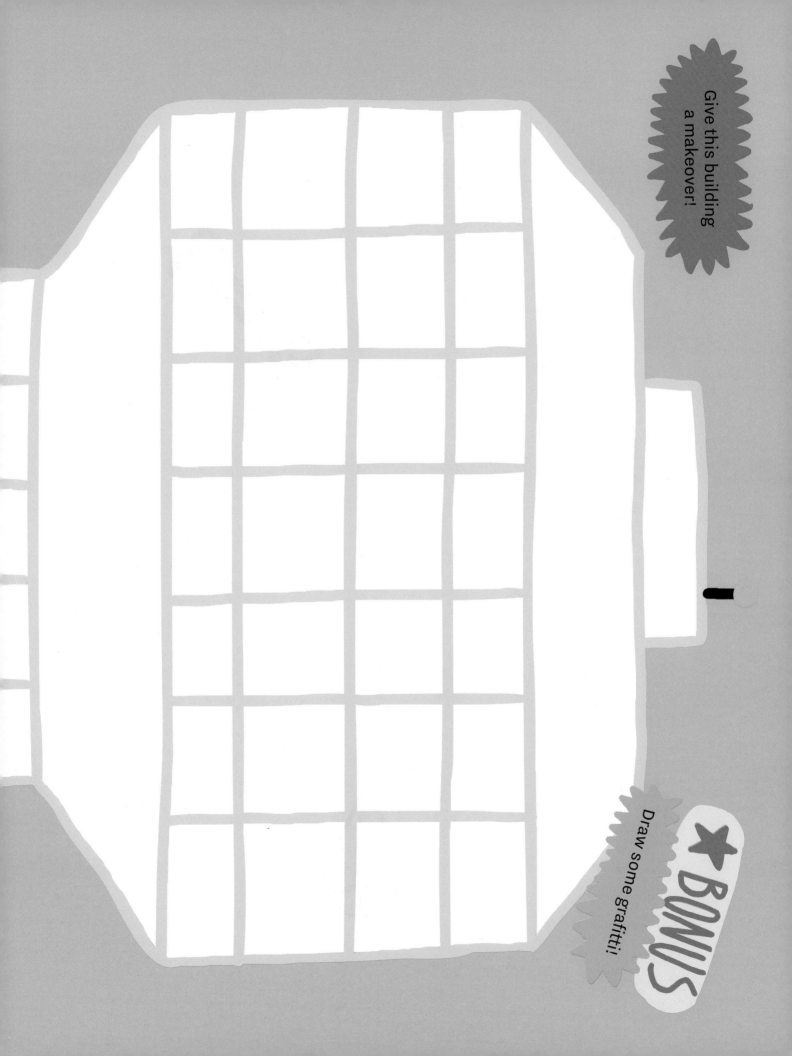

Give this building a makeover!

★ BONUS
Draw some grafitti!

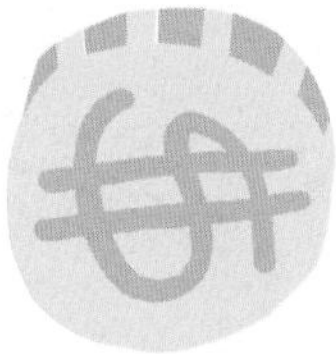

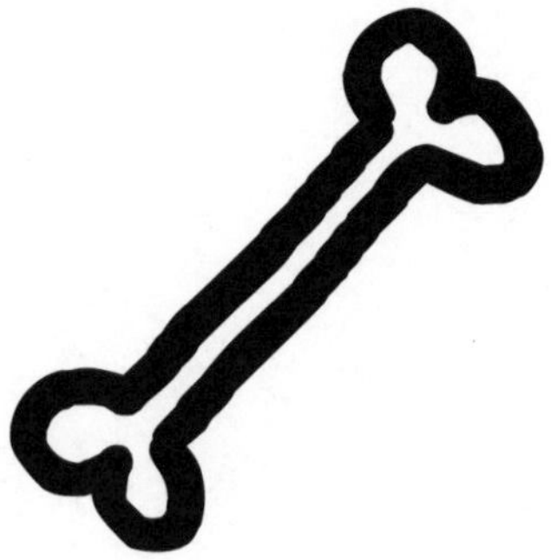

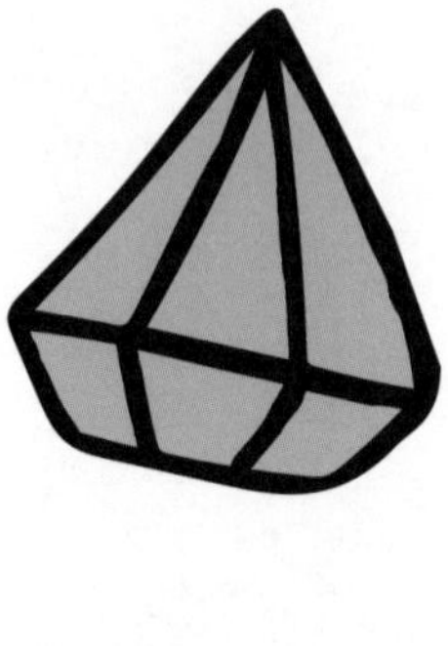

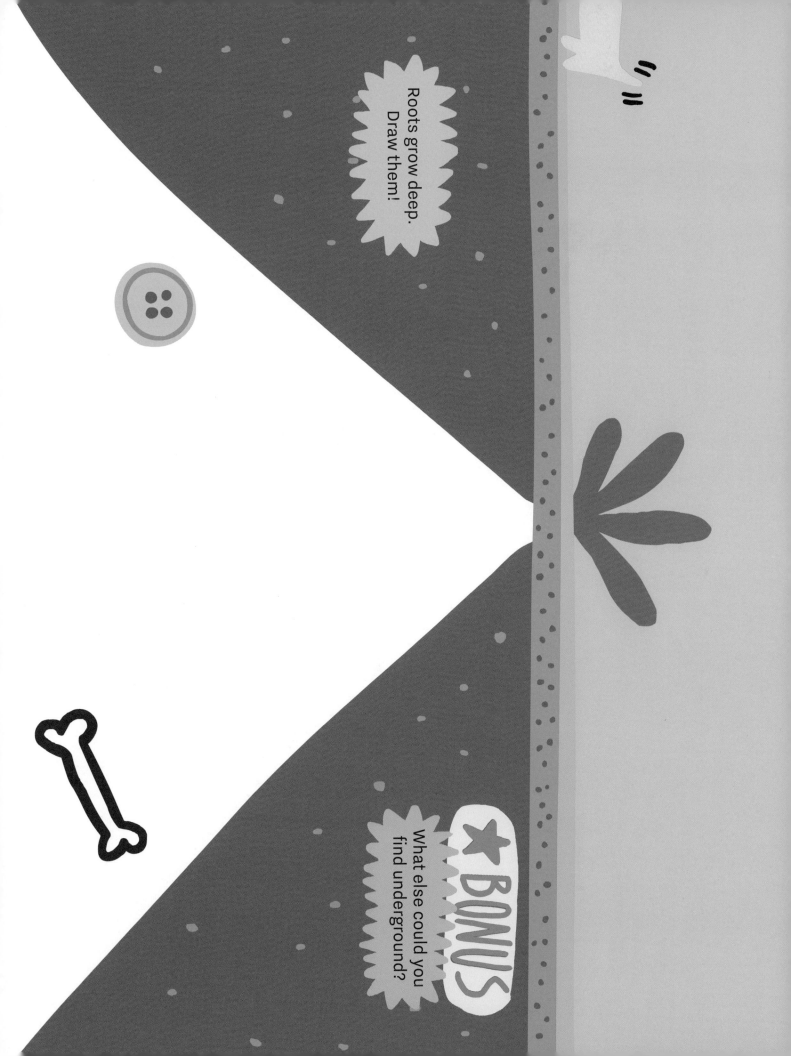

Roots grow deep.
Draw them!

★ BONUS

What else could you
find underground?

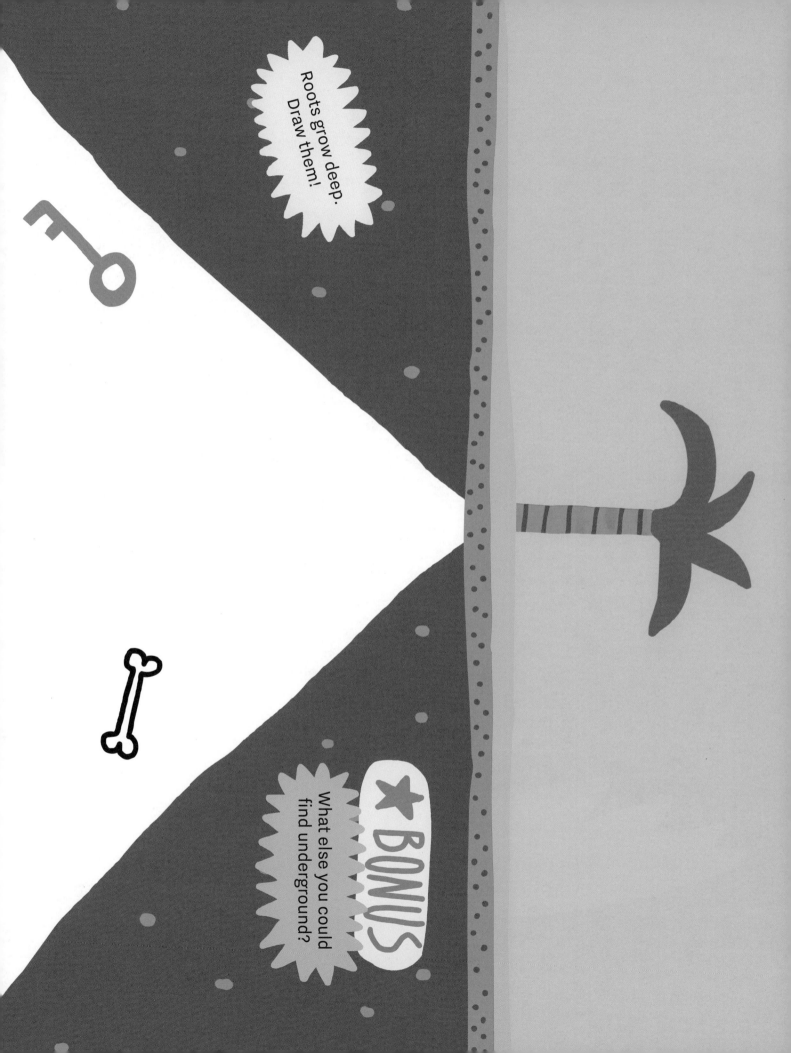

Roots grow deep. Draw them!

★ BONUS
What else you could find underground?

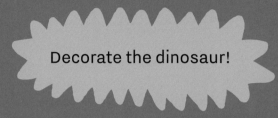

Decorate the dinosaur!

Draw your own dino!

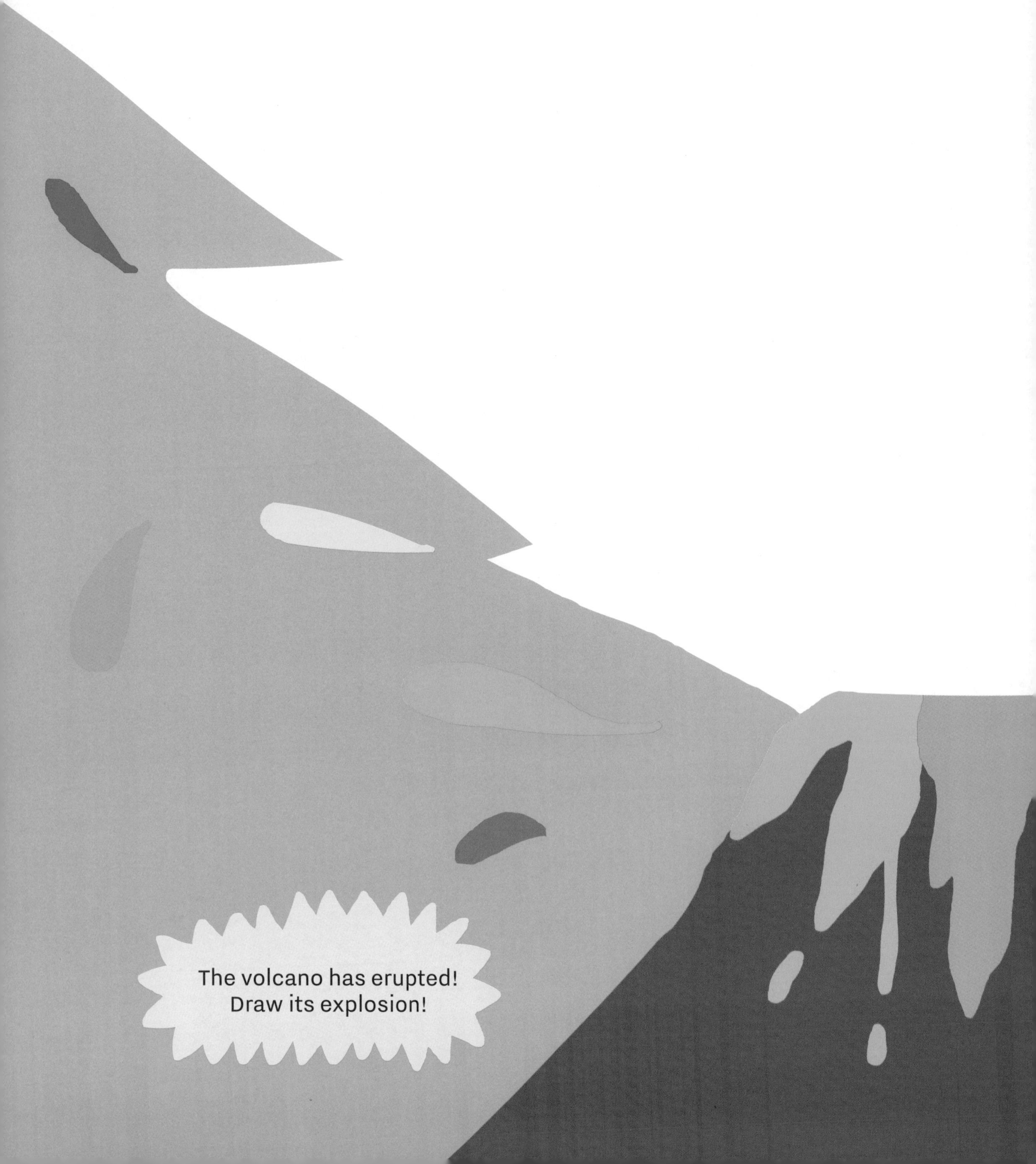
The volcano has erupted!
Draw its explosion!

What if a rainbow met a twister?

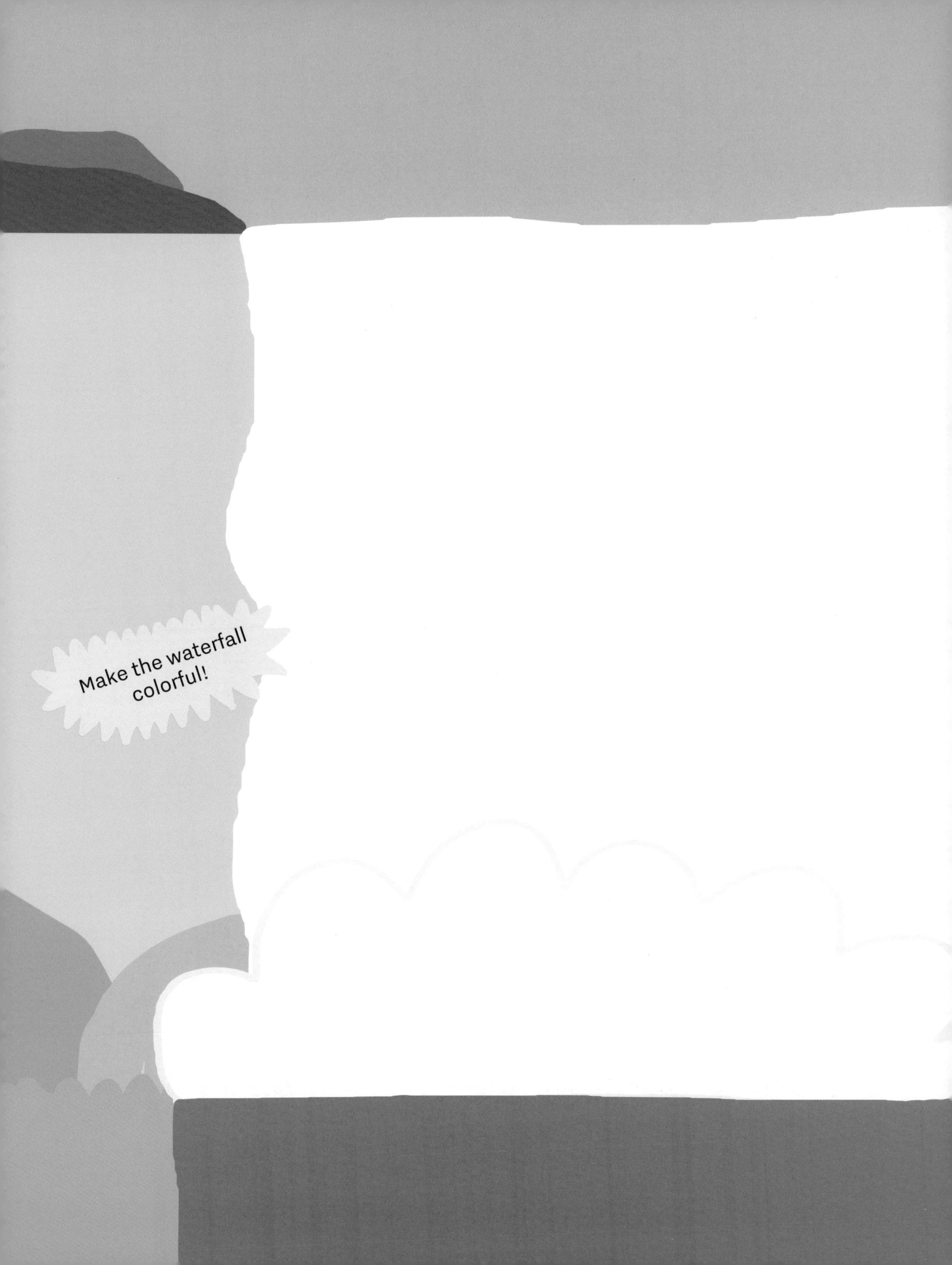
Make the waterfall colorful!

Design your own headgear!

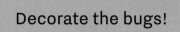

Make the insects shine, sparkle, and shimmer!

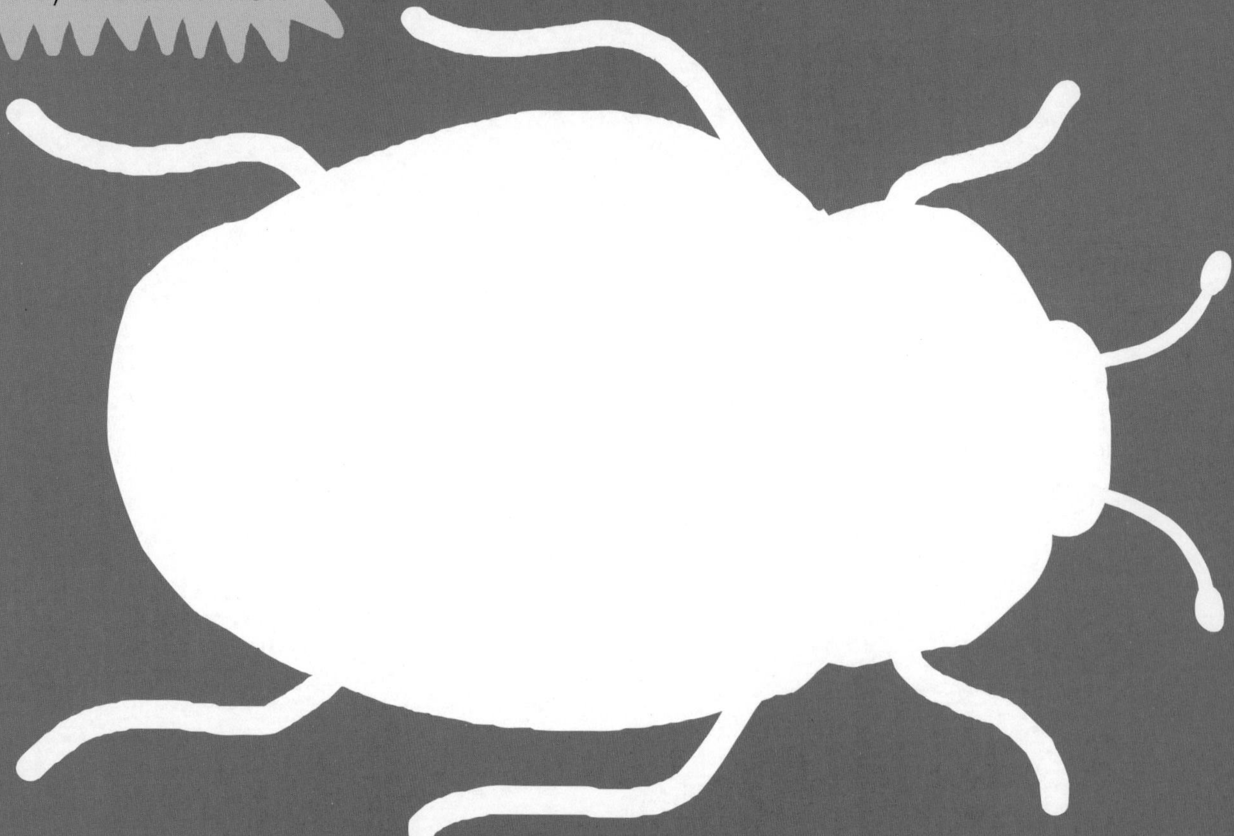

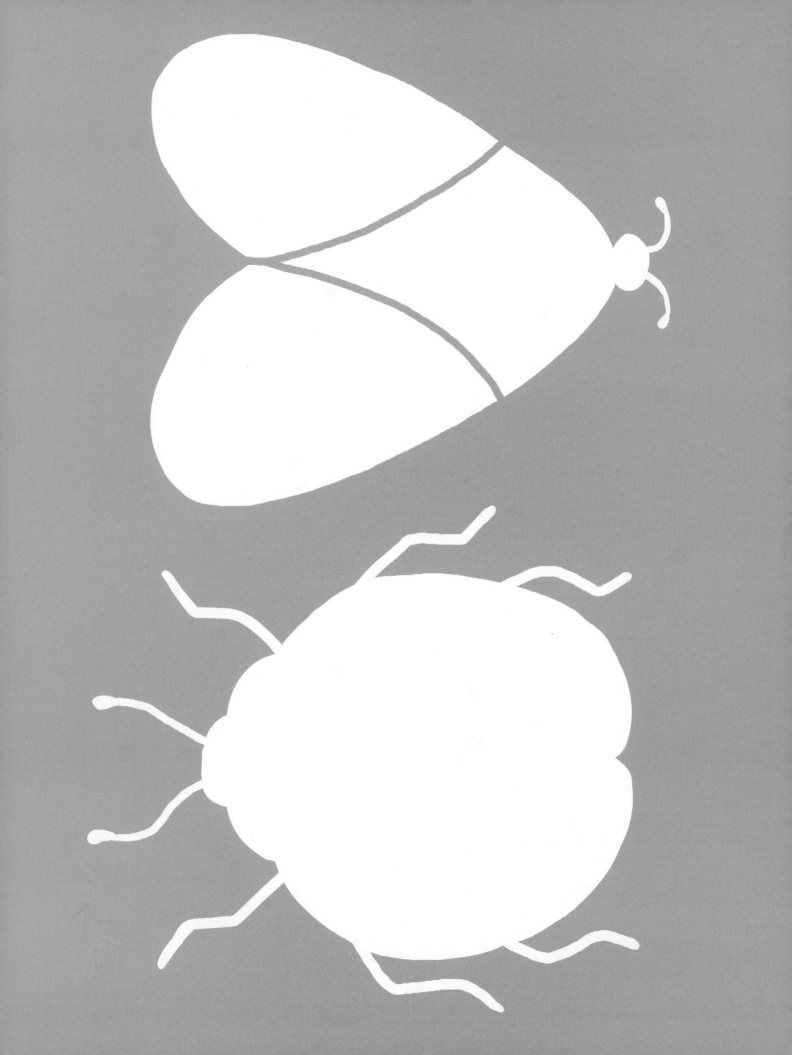

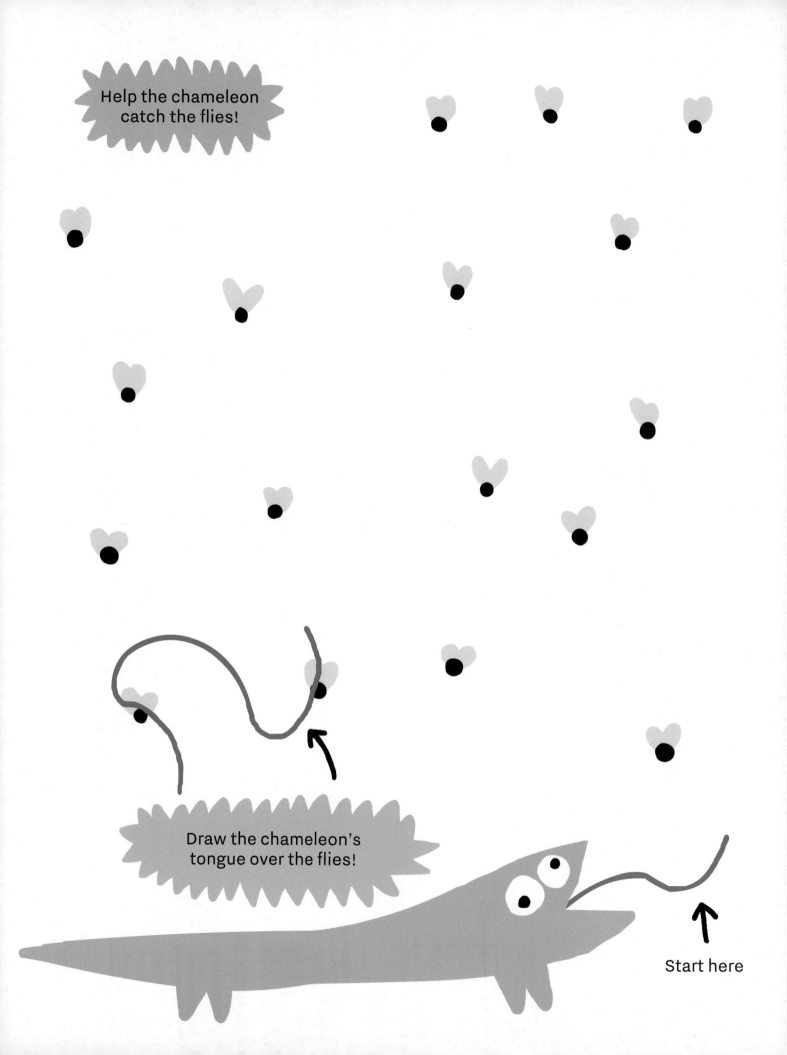

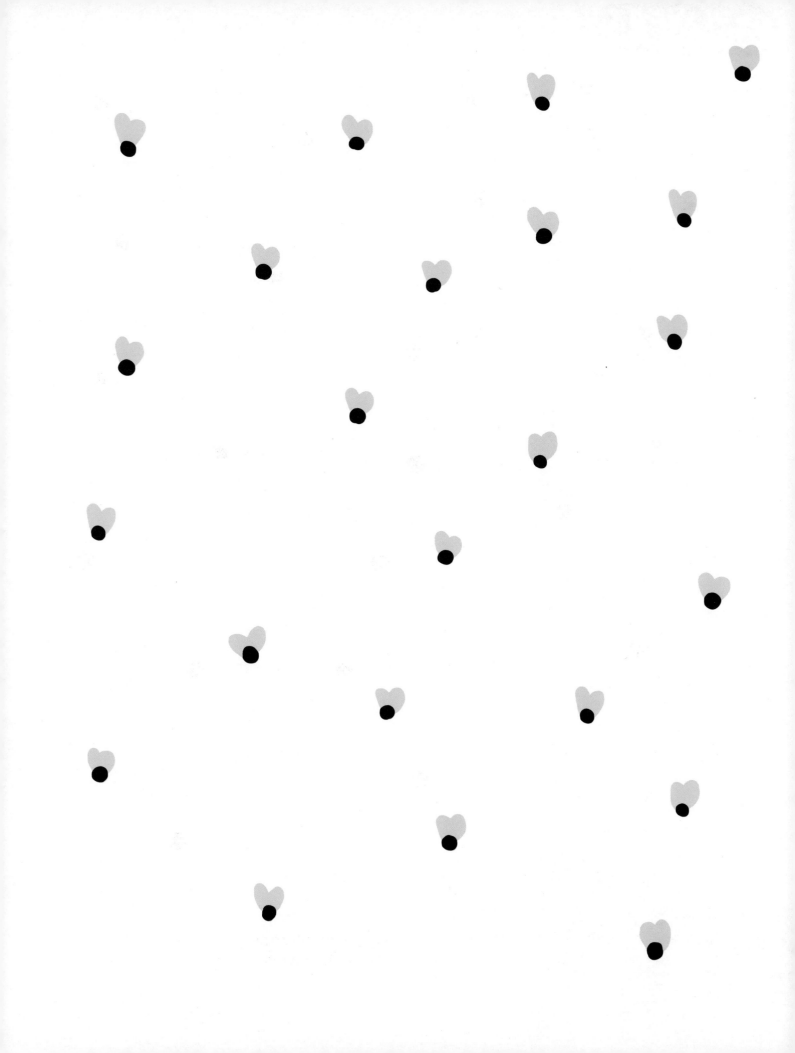

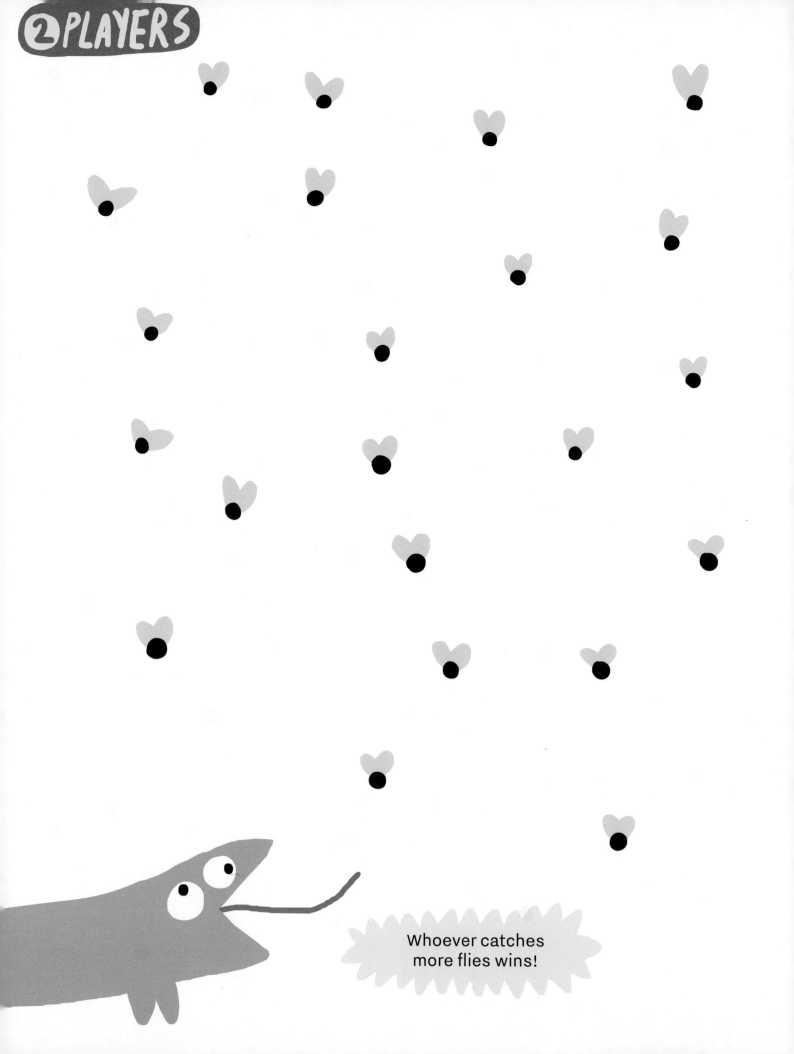

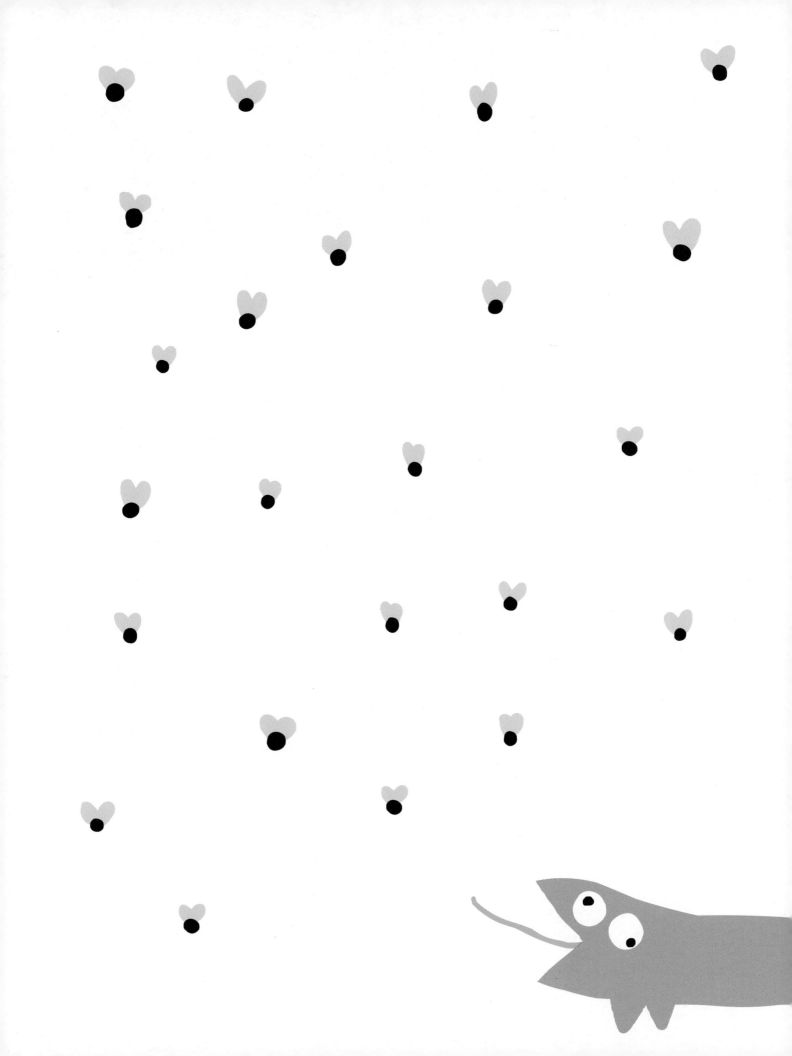

Make a storm of color. Avoid obstacles or draw more!

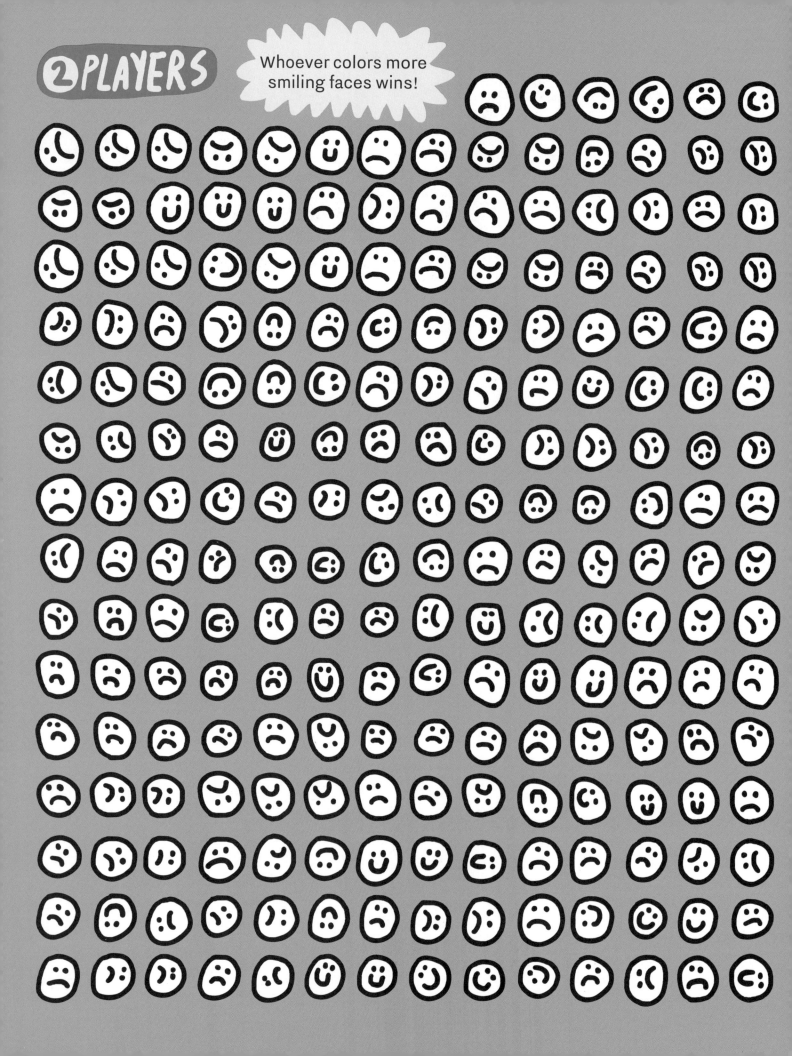

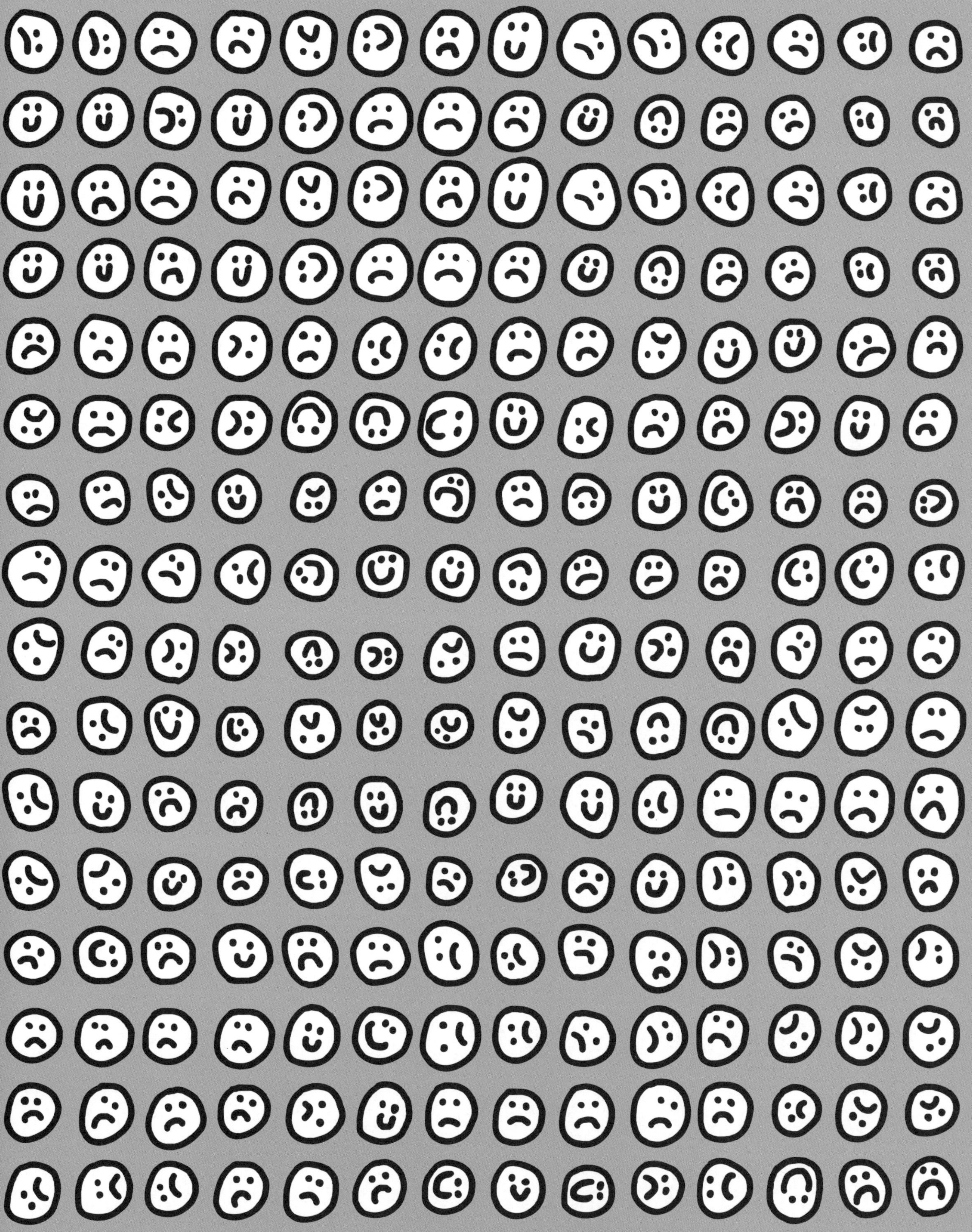

Punk haircuts!
Draw them wild!

What would your favorite
T-shirt look like?

★ BONUS

Create a logo
for your brand!

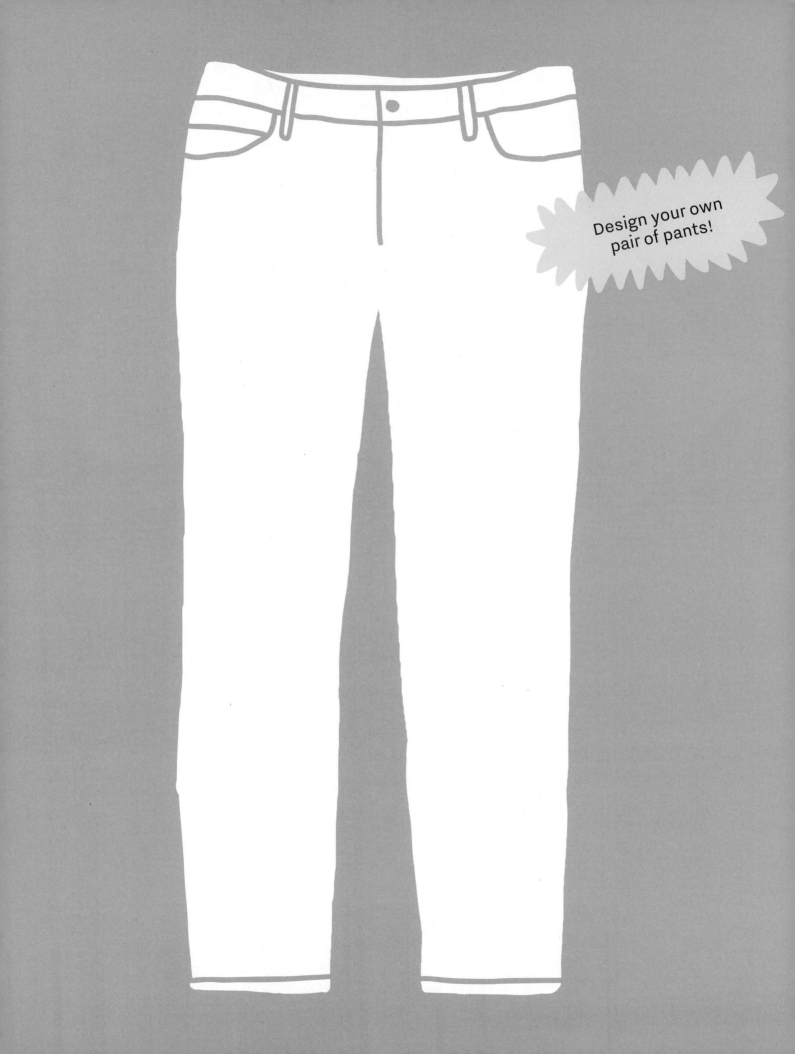

Design your own
pair of pants!

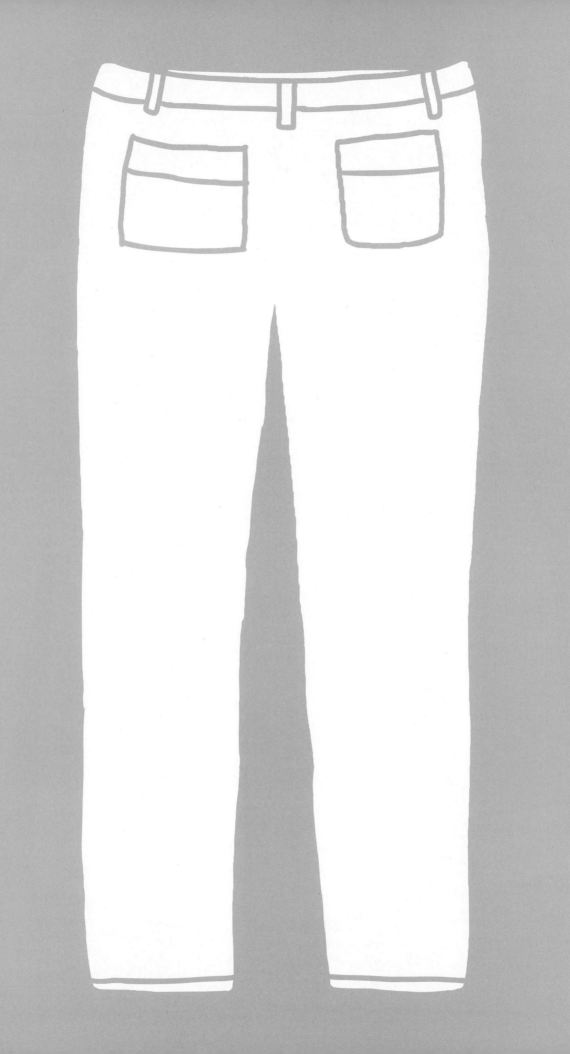

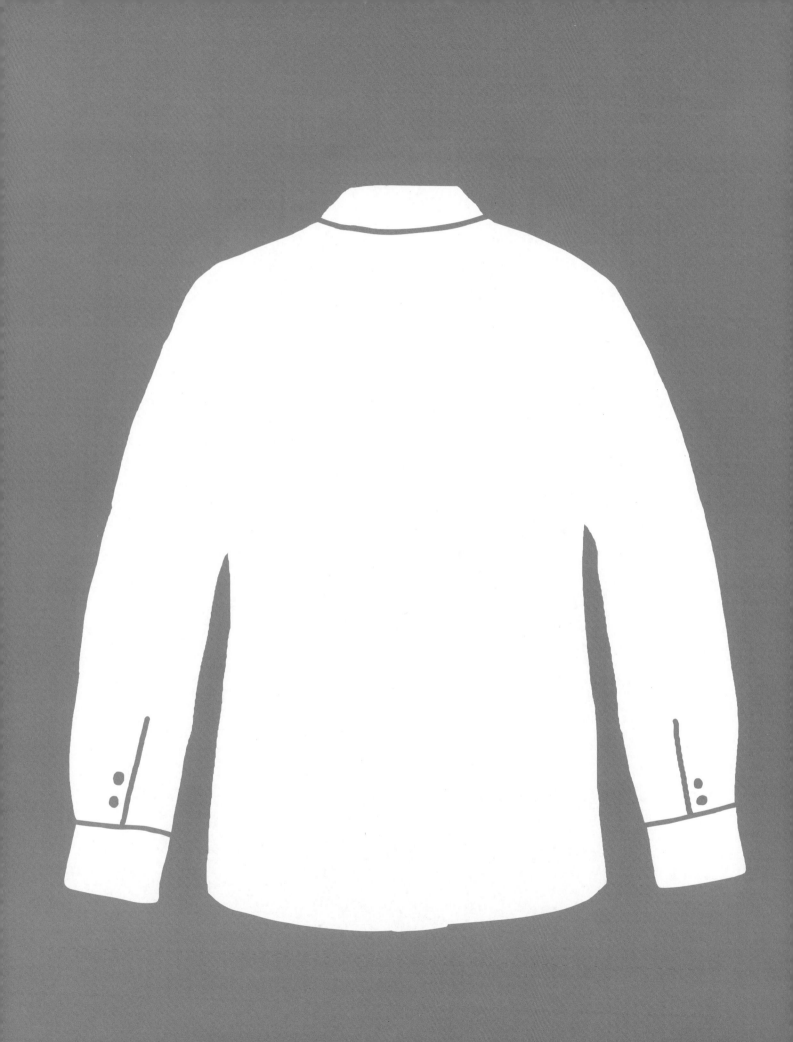

Imagine your own biker jacket.
Decorate as you wish!

★ BONUS

Draw pins and badges!

Decorate the bags!

Shampoo, toothpaste, and other stuff accidently came open inside the suitcase! What a mess!

Draw what spilled out!

Design some fancy bags!

Use scribbles as ingredients!

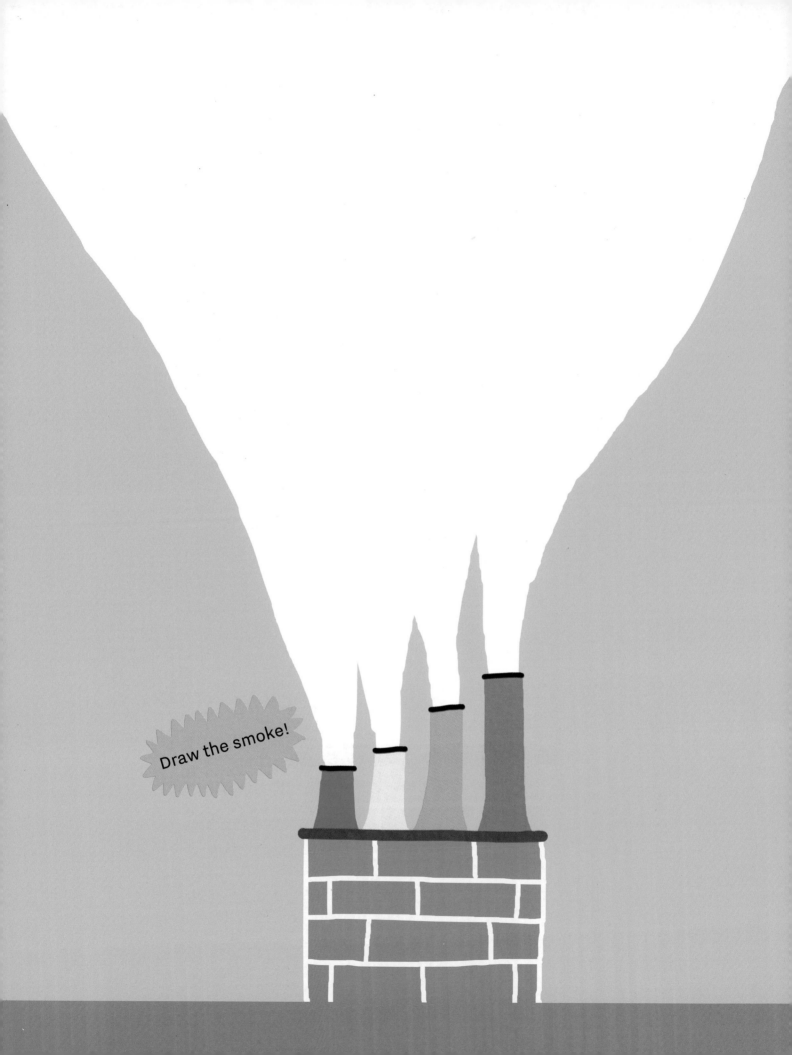

Birds are wonderful!
Draw your own!

Draw some fabulous feathers!

Draw some terrific monsters!

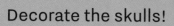

★ BONUS

Add some jewels
set in the skulls!

Decorate the masks!

★ BONUS

Add some jewels set in the masks!

Draw your masterpiece!

Draw the biggest, wackiest sculpture you can imagine!

Complete the chili peppers!

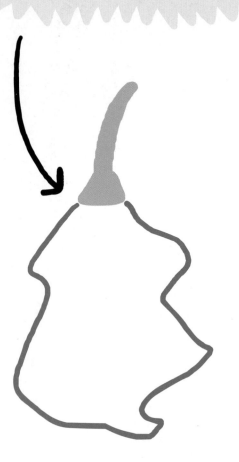

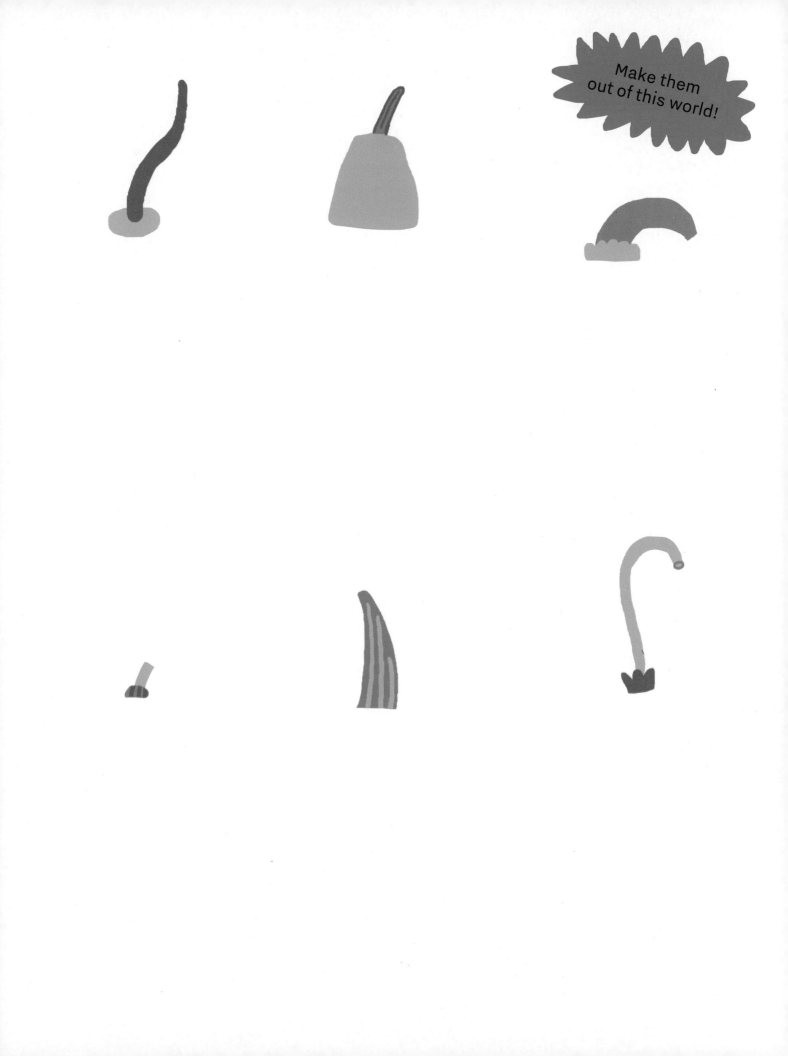

Make them out of this world!

Create the most delicious jam!

Use scribbles
as ingredients!

Create a poisoned jam!

What does the fastest car
in the world look like?
Draw it!

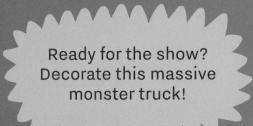
Ready for the show? Decorate this massive monster truck!

Ready for a road trip?
Decorate your family car!

Decorate the camper!
Have a nice trip!

Dive and do
a great stunt!

Make a big
splash too!

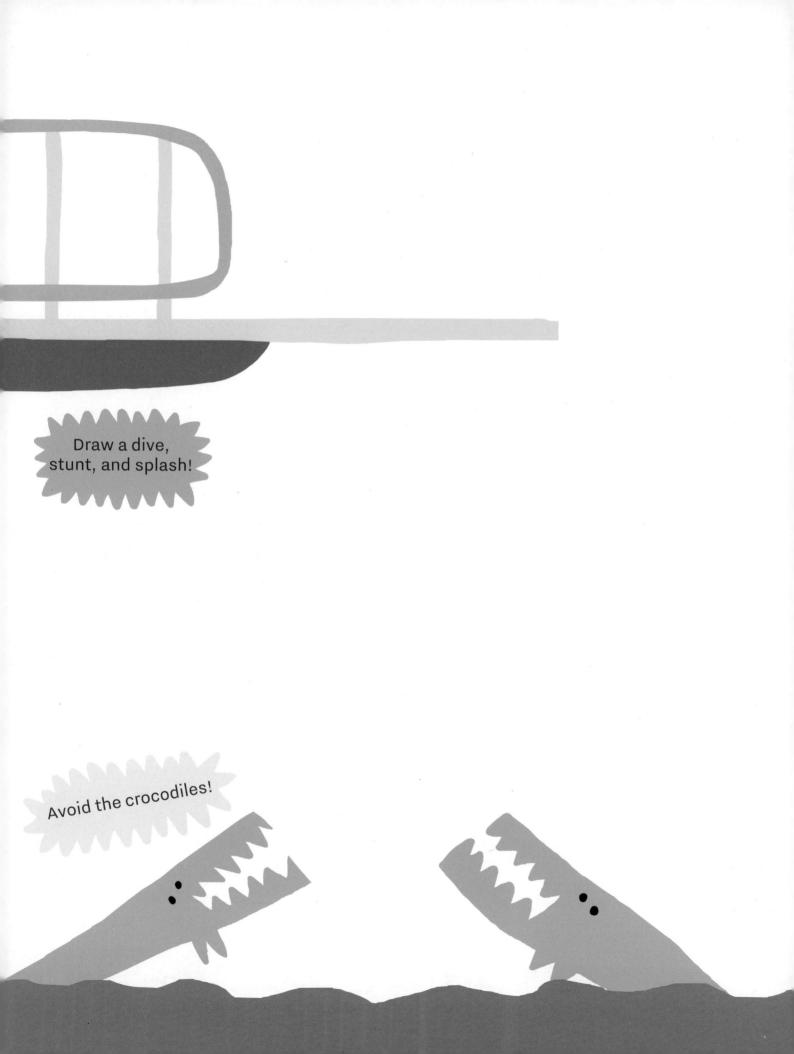

The higher the jump, the bigger the splash!

Dive and make
a great stunt!

Draw a scribbles-pizza!

Now draw a poisoned
scribbles-pizza!

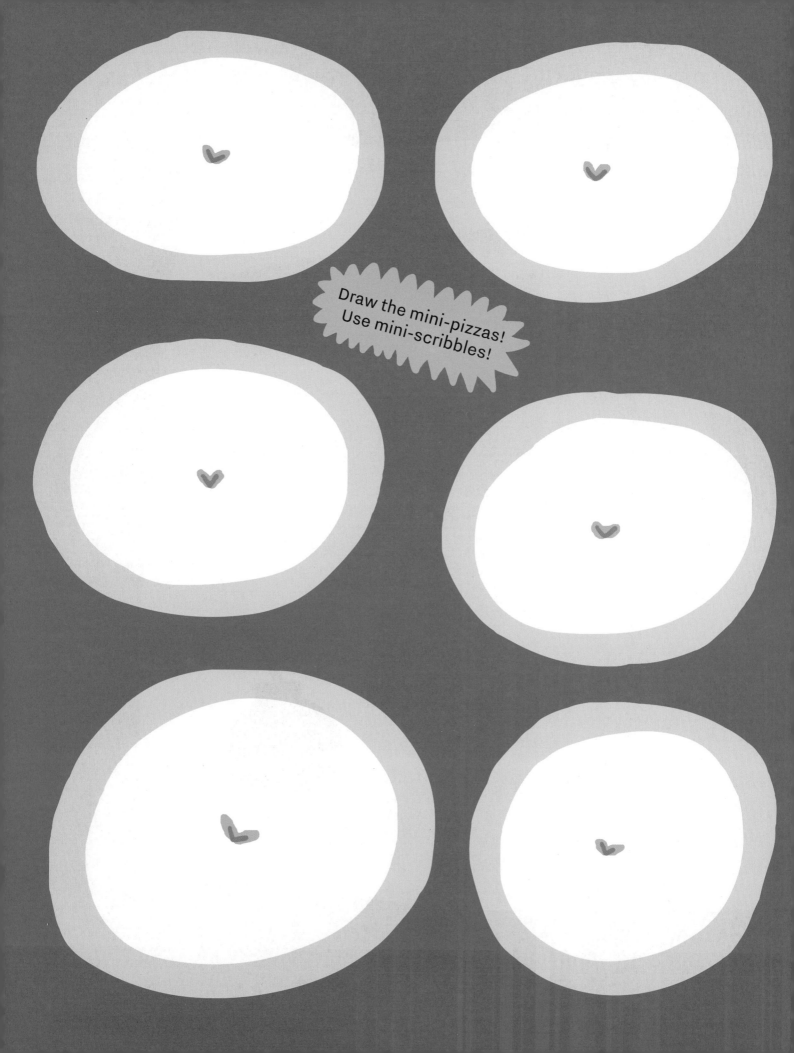

Draw the mini-pizzas!
Use mini-scribbles!

2 PLAYERS

Mustard vs. ketchup! Who will win?

Draw sauce all over the place!

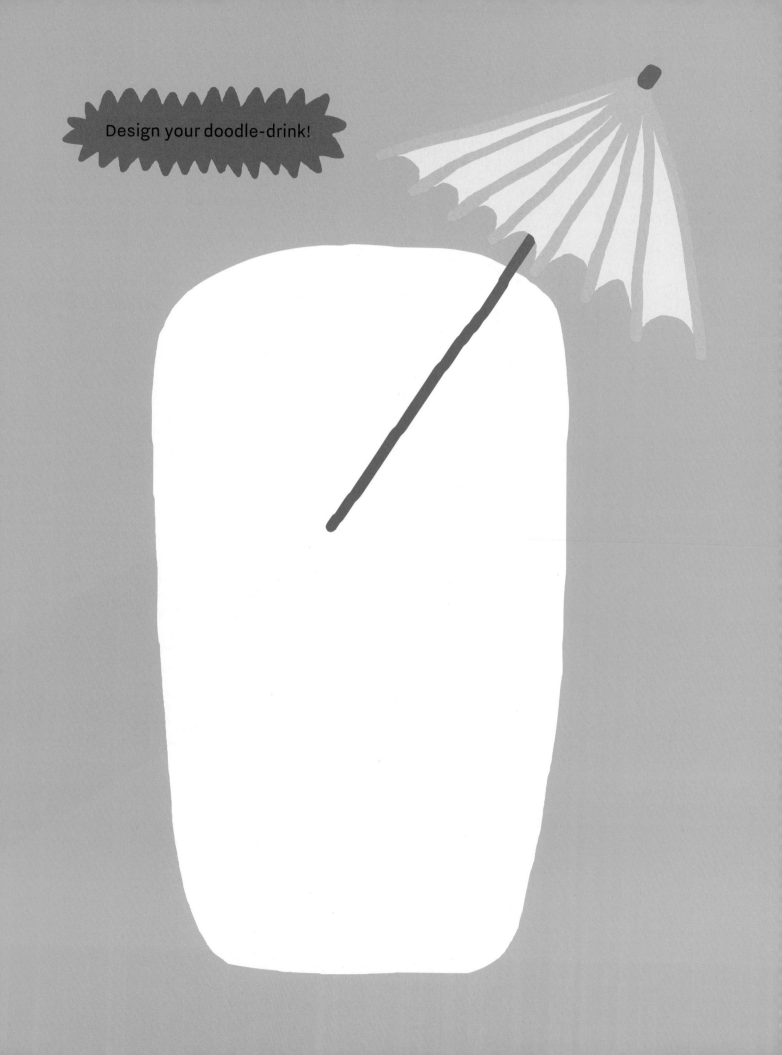

Design your doodle-drink!

Design your poisoned doodle-drink!

Stuff this sandwich with doodles!

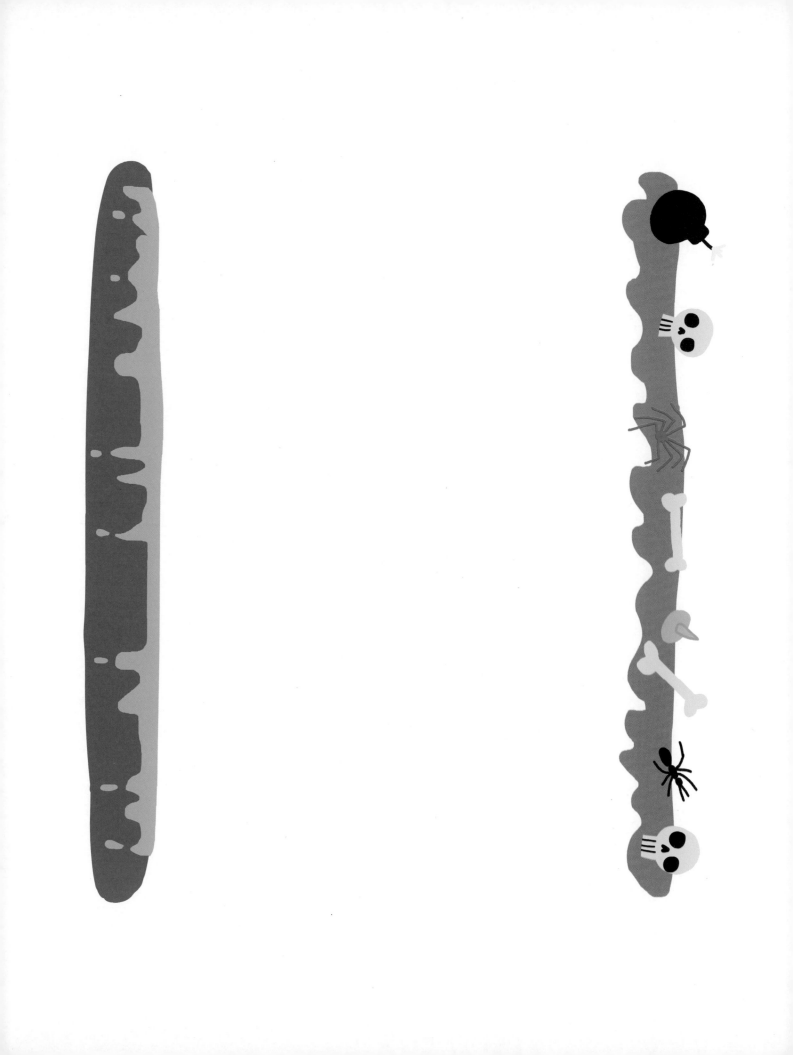

Draw a poisoned doodle-sandwich!

Extinguish the fire by doodling over it!

Odd Dot

An imprint of Macmillan Publishing Group, LLC

120 Broadway, New York, NY 10271

OddDot.com

Odd Dot® is a registered trademark of Macmillan Publishing Group, LLC

ISBN: 978-1-250-90098-2

DESIGNERS Christina Quintero and Caitlyn Hunter

EDITOR Justin Krasner

Our books are available at special discounts when purchased in bulk for premiums and sales promotions as well as for fund-raising or educational use. Special editions or book excerpts also can be created to specification. For details, contact the Macmillan Corporate and Premium Sales Department at (800) 221-7945 ext. 5442, or send an email to MacmillanSpecialMarkets@macmillan.com.

Printed in China by 1010 Printing International Limited, Kwun Tong, Hong Kong

First edition, 2024

1 3 5 7 9 10 8 6 4 2

Joyful Books for Curious Minds